RIC THORPE

Bishop of Islington

RESOURCE CHURCHES

A story of church planting and
revitalisation across the nation

the Gregory Centre for Church Multiplication
ccx.org.uk

RESOURCE CHURCHES

First published in 2021 by The Gregory Centre for Church Multiplication

St Edmund the King, Lombard Street, London, EC3V 9EA

www.ccx.org.uk

Editor Helen Cockram

Cover Design and typeset by Revo Creative Ltd

ISBN 978-1-8384-7430-0

eISBN 978-1-8384-7431-7

Printed in the United Kingdom

First Edition 2021
1 2 3 4 5 6 7 8 9 10

RESOURCE CHURCHES

Ric Thorpe represents a rare combination, being at once a thinker and strategist, and a practitioner. In his role as the Bishop of Islington, Ric is closely and centrally involved in the Church of England's aim to see all kinds of new churches planted. There is food for thought and inspiration here, and impetus for action.

MOST REVD AND RT HON JUSTIN WELBY, Archbishop of Canterbury

This book is an important contribution to our understanding of resource churches and the Church today. Not only does it describe resource churches in detail and depth, but it provides us with reflection and challenge. These stories of what God is doing give me hope and faith for the future of the gospel in our land.

RT REVD AND RT HON DAME SARAH MULLALY, Bishop of London

Bishop Ric Thorpe provides the definitive handbook on England's 100 Resource Churches. Ric supports his compelling theological and missiological reasons for such churches with authentic stories from different locations and traditions. It is a 'go to' book for parishes, diocesan teams and bishops.

MOST REVD AND RT HON STEPHEN COTTRELL, Archbishop of York

Resource churches have become an important part of the strategy for renewal of many dioceses across the country. This book is an invaluable guide to the history, nature, and potential of these churches to bring renewed life to cities, parishes and the different traditions of the Church of England in the coming years.

RT REVD DR GRAHAM TOMLIN, Bishop of Kensington

Bishop Ric Thorpe writes on church planting with authority and experience. As the first ever national bishop for church planting in the Church of England he has seen new church communities grow and flourish all over the country through a combination of dynamic leadership and the Spirit of God. I hope this inspiring book will encourage the launch of many more such initiatives.

REVD NICKY GUMBEL, Vicar of Holy Trinity Brompton, London

Such a helpful book! Resource Churches have attracted a lot of attention but little balanced reflection. What often goes unnoticed are the great variety of models and approaches, the historical precedents, and the combination of visionary leadership and sacrificial generosity that is involved in extending the Church's mission in these ways.

REVD PAUL HARCOURT, National Leader, New Wine England

Clear, humble, generous, honest. A must-read for anyone involved in resource church planting.

RT REVD DR JILL DUFF, Bishop of Lancaster

Resource churches and church planting are vital for the renewal of the whole Anglican tradition, reaching new populations and young people, who find in them opportunities for discipleship and social engagement. Be encouraged by these stories of real people in real places who are keeping the rumour of God alive.

RT REVD DR JOANNE GRENFELL, Bishop of Stepney

This is a deeply encouraging book, and encouraging on so many levels. It tells real-life stories about churches growing, developing, engaging, learning, and planting... and does so in a way that lets us begin to dream that we can do this too. It engages with the challenges realistically and honestly, because church growth isn't always easy... and yet usually has a sparkle in the eye that is reflected on the pages of this book. It asks good questions, theologically, structurally, and practically. It is rooted both in faith and a deep commitment to share the love of Christ. It spans traditions, geography, and social context. Read it! Read it carefully, read it joyfully, read it inquisitively... and expect neither that you will leave unchanged, nor that you will have a magic formula to employ. For God is at work in his church and his world, and this is part of what he is up to.

RT REVD MARK TANNER, Bishop of Chester

The term 'resource church' has been bandied around in Church of England circles for some 8 years or more, but now with this book we have clarity around the what, why and how of such churches, explained carefully and practically, and accompanied by hugely encouraging case studies. This is both a reference book and a faith-builder for any diocese and church leader.

REVD ARCHIE COATES, Vicar of St Peter's Brighton

As a planter, supporter of practitioners, overseer and now author, Bishop Ric shows us in word and deed how Jesus continues to take all we offer and multiplies it many times over so many more can be fed. The focus isn't solving a problem in the church but the renewal of the world by God's transforming love. This gem of a book has been forged in the reality of experience, is rich in theology, full of practical wisdom and valuable to anyone keen to see how God is at work through resource churches.

REVD BARRY HILL, Leicester Diocese Resource Church Enabler and Team Rector of Market Harborough

Straight from the horse's mouth—this primer on British church planting covers both the theology and recent history of the strategic revitalisation of the Church of England. Having played a key role in the establishing of one hundred resource churches (so far), I can think of no one more qualified than Ric Thorpe to guide us on this important journey.

REVD DR CHRISTIAN SELVARATNAM, Director of the St Hild Centre for Church Planting

Throughout the whole adventure of planting Gas Street Church in Birmingham, Bishop Ric has been a constant source of encouragement and support. He has pushed us to think bigger and provided strategic input to help us navigate particular obstacles along the way. This is an exciting, important and necessary book that captures all of Ric's vision and wisdom.

REVD TIM HUGHES, Vicar of Gas Street Church Birmingham

This book is a must for anybody considering church planting. Ric is a fountain of knowledge and wisdom on the theology, the history and the practice of planting churches that reach our communities. This is a brilliant and helpful resource.

REVD MIKE PILAVACHI, Soul Survivor Watford

Ric Thorpe has assembled a compendium of stories of hope for Church and nation. These dazzling accounts of the work of the Holy Spirit, passing on the baton of faith received from the apostles, also prompt us to recognise dependence on God who speaks in stillness and silence.

RT REVD DR AND RT HON MARTIN WARNER, Bishop of Chichester

The call to make disciples is from the Lord Jesus. When disciples gather for nurturing and are further discipled, the assembly of disciples is called 'church'. The setting-up or recognition of the resource church is crucial and important for every diocese. It is the driving force, training centre, focal point for mission-sending and resource-sharing for the revitalisation or new church plants. Bishop Ric Thorpe has certainly captured the essence of the resource church, including its theological understanding, the practicalities and challenges.

RT REVD MOON HING NG, formerly Archbishop of South East Asia

I have long been of the view that we needed a new form of church in Newcastle Diocese, and the resource church has fulfilled the hopes we've had for it from the beginning, with a new kind of reaching out. We are delighted with the results – the addition of a resource church enriches us as a diocese, and I believe that resource churches fit well into the wider scope of the Church.

RT REVD AND RT HON CHRISTINE HARDMAN, Bishop of Newcastle

When Bishop Ric challenged some of us Anglican church leaders to think about a new resource church in Bradford, we knew, whatever models were being tried out elsewhere, that the resource church had to be truly 'Bradford'. For us, that meant young, entrepreneurial, and diverse. It meant the church investing into the city's vision of renewal, growth, and well-being, with an offer of the abundant life that God offers to us in Jesus. We are delighted that our new church affirms the diversity of the city while calling people to follow Christ.

RT REVD DR TOBY HOWARTH, Bishop of Bradford

For us to be able to reinvigorate struggling city-centre churches with a resourcing team intent on communicating in every way the joy of the gospel, focused strongly on evangelism and sacrificial in its service of the poor, can only be good news.

RT REVD PHILIP NORTH, Bishop of Burnley

One of the contributions made by the resource church programme was a realisation that a much more intentional approach to growth was needed across the whole of our city. It is still early days and we are learning all the time, but we have five resource churches across Leeds and a number of small plants and substantial plants either completed, or well on the way.

RT REVD PAUL SLATER, Bishop of Kirkstall (Area Bishop for the city of Leeds)

This book has made me restless for more. More churches, more Christians, but most of all, more of God. This is a compelling and inspiring read, with so many great stories and so much practical wisdom all in one place. I highly recommend this for all archdeacons. A hugely inspiring read whatever your tradition.

VEN RHIANNON KING, Archdeacon of Ipswich and Director of Inspiring Ipswich

The diversity of local context and opportunity means careful discernment and a mixed ecology in the way we set about our missional task. Today, church planting through resource churches is one effective means to that end. We can no longer rely on one model of church, namely the parish, if we want to see growth. We need innovation. Developing resource churches is demanding of energy and leadership on all concerned, but I am convinced it is worth it.

RT REVD PETER HILL, Bishop of Barking

Bishop Ric's commitment to church planting and growth is infectious, visionary, and yet wonderfully practical. This book helps us all to see what is being achieved, and challenges us to raise our own sights as we seek to present and grow into Christ in our different localities.

RT REVD ROD THOMAS, Bishop of Maidstone

All churches were once 'planted churches', as Christianity spread. Bishop Ric has shown the value of planting and reviving churches. This book tells inspiring stories of the renewed spread of the faith, through new and revived churches across many of the towns and cities of England.

WILLIAM NYE, General Secretary of the Church of England

This is an exciting, informative, passionate book giving the story, theology and vision around resource churches by one of the best leaders I know. You can't read it without being inspired that this current move sits in the long history of the Holy Spirit at work through the followers of Jesus, to the glory of God.

REVD GARETH ROBINSON, Rector of St Philips Chapel Street, Salford, and Head of church planting training for New Wine England; author of *Stones & Ripples: Ten Principles for Pioneers and Church Planters*

Thoughtful, practical, and wise, this book is the guide to the resource church so many have been waiting for.

REVD MATTHEW PORTER, Vicar of St Michael le Belfrey in York; author of *Overflow*

We have been delighted to help enable the development of a resource church in our diocese, especially as its inception came from the local congregation listening to God and reimagining their future. This is a fabulous example of bottom-up discernment and prophetic wisdom.

RT REVD ROB WICKHAM, Bishop of Edmonton

This book captures new journeys of faith that Bishop Ric has championed, including the Catholic renewal at St George-in-the-East. I hope and pray these stories are a springboard for others too.

FR RICHARD SPRINGER, Rector of St George-in-the-East

Resourcing churches are a vital – though not exclusive – plank in our commitment to reach people with the good news of Jesus Christ. I am more than ever convinced of the important part that resourcing churches can play, alongside parish churches, in the renewal and growth of the Church and the spread of the gospel. I value resource churches and also working with the Spirit so as to adapt the vision for individual circumstances. Our particular example of resource church has not turned out as I would have predicted: it's much more exciting!

RT REVD DR AND RT HON JOHN INGE, Bishop of Worcester

This book is a timely and important contribution to the essential work of church planting in the UK. It is helpfully set out, outlining church planting theory, history and theology, interspersed with stories of church plants. These real examples bring to life the joys and challenges of church planting and invite the exploration of different ways of approaching the task. There are helpful frameworks for resource churches, dioceses and churches wanting to form new worshipping communities. Bishop Ric brings his personal experience of planting together with the wisdom he's gathered through networking with leaders from different traditions and streams. It will be an invaluable resource for anyone involved in church planting in the UK today.

REVD VICTORIA RAMSEY, Diocesan Church Growth and Planting Enabler, Diocese of Southwell & Nottingham

This is a story that really needed to be told, and Ric Thorpe is the one to tell it. Inspiring, theologically-grounded and practically useful, Ric shares the story-so-far of how resource churches have brought about the revitalisation of churches and the transformation of communities across the UK.

RT REVD RUTH BUSHYAGER, Bishop of Horsham

CONTENTS

ACKNOWLEDGEMENTS

I could not have written this book without the help of many, many people.

First of all, I want to thank Louie, my wife, who has been an amazing tower of strength, encouragement and patience throughout the writing of this book, and to our children, Zoe, Barny and Toby. You keep me pointing towards Jesus and his Kingdom and you keep me down to earth!

I want to thank all the bishops who have contributed to this book. You are creating space for something new and fanning it into flame and it is exciting to see where this is leading. Thanks especially to Archbishop Justin Welby for writing the foreword and Bishop Sarah Mullally for the afterword – thank you for your encouragement and courage in supporting me with this work. Thanks too to the resource church leaders who have told their stories in these pages. Thank you for your courage, faith, generosity and tenacity – you are an inspiration!

I am so grateful to those who have inspired and influenced my thinking in this work. Thanks to Bishop Sandy Millar, for the time and love you have poured into me over years. I caught this from you. Thank you to Nicky Gumbel, Miles Toulmin, Tricia Neill and Mark Elsdon-Dew for your friendship and for building strong foundations for others to build on. To Bishop Richard Chartres, thank you for believing in me and always encouraging me. To Philip James and the Strategic Development Unit in Church House Westminster, thank you for the extraordinary behind-the-scenes work you do, serving the Church, and for the data and rigour you give to supporting dioceses. Thank you too to the leaders and people of St Paul's Shadwell, St Peter's Bethnal Green, All Hallows Bow, St Luke's Millwall and Christchurch Spitalfields, who helped develop so much of my own thinking by your prayers, ambitious faith and generosity in seeing the Kingdom of God advance.

Thank you to those who have helped me actually write this book: to the Gregory Centre team and associates for praying, encouraging and supporting in various ways – you are an amazing team. Thank you, Winfield Bevins, for your huge encouragement and help, and the Beeston Scholarship Programme at Asbury Theological Seminary who enabled the doctoral work underpinning this book. Special thanks to Pete Broadbent, Mark Elsdon-Dew, Barry Hill, Angus Ritchie, Christian Selvaratnam, John Valentine and Lizzy Woolf for your insightful comments and reading drafts, to Philippa Guy for helping with the case studies, to Jo Stockdale and Julia Barbour for proofreading, to Toria Gray for overseeing and organising the production and to Emily Thomas for help with marketing. I am grateful to Helen Cockram for months of encouragement and editing, and to Andrea Bleakley for all the ways you support me administratively.

The story of resource churches told in this book would not have happened without the faithful prayers and radical commitment of all those passionate about seeing the kingdom of God reach new people in new places in new ways. Let the story continue!

FOREWORD

Justin Welby, Archbishop of Canterbury

I believe in the Church.

I believe in the Church because I believe in God who is Father, Son and Holy Spirit. And this Church looks both backwards and forwards. There are essential things that we all share. And there are particular things that mark each community as distinct.

One of the most hope-giving developments of the last decades in the Church of England has been the re-commitment to Church. Not for its own sake, but for the sake of this country that we are called to serve. This recommitment to Church has taken many forms, one such form is resource churches.

Whilst some might wonder how such churches fit within traditional Anglican ecclesiology, my sense is that they are deeply Anglican – borne out of a renewed commitment that the Church of England should be the Church for England. In 2015 there were just six resource churches, and today there are more than a hundred. They are of many different types, in many different areas around the country, in many different contexts. Behind each one is a story of vision, sacrifice, service and hope. And for all that has been given by so many I am truly grateful.

These churches are having a profound impact in the cities, towns and regions which they serve. They are also having an impact in the life of the church, with innovative and creative approaches to mission and ministry, collaborating across cities, regions and dioceses. There are swathes of new (usually young) leaders offering themselves for ordination and leadership in the church of Jesus Christ. I find all of this profoundly encouraging. However, perhaps most encouraging of all are the testimonies of people finding faith in Jesus Christ through the witness of these churches, often from demographics and backgrounds which have been sadly missing from our churches. There are literally hundreds, even thousands, of people coming to faith in Jesus Christ around the country through the mission and ministry of resource churches.

I have known Ric Thorpe now for over 10 years. He represents a rare combination, being at once a thinker and strategist, and a practitioner. Ric and his wife Louie have planted several churches in London's East End over a 10-year period. Now, in his role as the Bishop of Islington, he is closely and centrally involved in the Church of England's aim to see all kinds of new churches planted in new places in new ways to reach new people. Of course, some of this work feels risky, but God has used Bishop Ric's experience and faith to inspire confidence and hope. None of this is without its challenges, but there is now a clear track record of churches being raised and witnessing powerfully in cities and regions to the love of God. This raises our faith, courage and confidence that the Good News of the Kingdom of God is transforming the lives of individuals and communities and bearing fruit in our nation.

I remain convinced that the hope, that is ours because the Father raised his Son Jesus Christ from the grave in the power of the Holy Spirit, lies behind this phenomenon of church planting, and the establishing of resource churches. In this book Ric does us the service of leading us through the biblical and theological background to what we are seeing, and traces resource churches through the Christian history of our country. Here we understand that resource churches are not a new thing, but part of an ancient ecclesiology and practice. And they are a great cause for hope as we look to the future.

I am often asked if I have hope for the Church of England. And unhesitatingly I answer yes. The reason I have hope is because of God. And the amazing stories that make up a fair proportion of this book are testimony to the beauty of God's ways. I love those stories of bishops, senior teams, church leaders and church planters working together for the sake of those they are called to serve and love. It is exciting to read of individual lives being transformed by Jesus, and communities becoming aware of his kingdom. And it is encouraging to read the clear and well thought-through steps that mark the road which has seen the establishment of these resource churches. I praise God for these signs of the work of the Holy Spirit in our day.

So, may I encourage you to read, and to do so with faith and hope? There is food for thought and inspiration here, and impetus for action. Churches and their leaders, other denominations, and Christians from all round the world have expressed a desire to learn from these resource churches. Of course, they are not the only answer to the challenges which the church of Jesus Christ faces in twenty-first century Britain, but they do seem to me to be a gift which every part of the Church can learn from, be encouraged by, and join in with.

INTRODUCTION – BLUE SKY DREAMS

It was a warm sunny day in October 2008 in an out-of-season hotel on the Portuguese coast. We were standing around a flip chart with a rough drawing of England covered in crosses marking churches in various locations, with lines and arrows going from them to other places nearby. I was part of a learning community, organised by Leadership Network as part of the European Church Planting Network, as a guest of the Holy Trinity Brompton (HTB) team with my former vicar, Bishop Sandy Millar.[1] We were dreaming dreams about how the Church of England could play its part in seeing the lives of people in our cities and towns transformed by the radical love of Jesus Christ, to reverse the church's decline and move into significant growth. We dreamed of churches multiplying, beginning in cities and planting and revitalising churches all across their regions, igniting a fire of renewal across the nation.

That map, and what came from it, are the foundations of what is written in this book. We didn't call them resource churches then, and HTB had not planted outside London at that stage, but what we had drawn were four city-centre churches, planted to resource their regions by planting churches that would in turn go on to plant other churches. It was a radical vision, and it took four more years for HTB to plant those first four churches. Fast forward another eight years and that dream is becoming a reality, with 100 resource churches from different networks in almost every diocese, planting or set up to plant and revitalise churches across their regions.

This book is about these resource churches. It tells the extraordinary story of what they are and how they have grown. I explore where they might be rooted theologically and historically. I explain how they are created, how they plant and revitalise churches, and how they develop leaders for this specific kind of church. I deal with some of the objections that have been raised and the obstacles they encounter, and look at some alternative models that have sprung up. And I suggest where this might all be heading, while acknowledging that we are in the very early stages of understanding how this is revitalising the Church. In between each chapter, I have included stories of specific resource churches, told by their leaders, and reflected on by their bishops. There is not enough space to tell all of the great stories that are emerging from these churches, but these stories and reflections are ways of describing what God is doing, and they all play a part in shaping and enriching our theology.

There are many ways to use this book. It is a kind of primer on the concept of resource churches. You can read it from start to finish and you will be taken on a logical journey. You can head straight for particular chapters that are relevant to you or that you want to find out more about. You can even use it as a workbook to help you think through the practical steps required to establish resource churches where you are. There will be more resources to help you apply all this on the Gregory Centre for Church Multiplication website, detailed at the back of this book. You could just read the exciting variety of stories. Or you can use it to prop up a broken chair. Something for everyone, I hope!

One of the things I love reminding myself is what Jesus thinks about the church. We're his people who are growing to know him and follow him and point others to him, more and more, day by day. We're his family united in beautiful diversity as brothers and sisters in Christ. We're his body, each playing a vital part. We're a holy temple in which he lives by his Spirit. We're his bride, who he loves, who he has forgiven and cleansed and made new, and he is preparing us to be with him forever. These beautiful images describe a little of how precious the Church is to him. So, in a way, this book is about calling the Church to be what he wants it to be. I am sure there are things I have written that need improving or correcting, but my desire is for us to be the best we can for Jesus.

We're his family united in beautiful diversity as brothers and sisters in Christ

So why this particular book? I have written this book to document the development of resource churches so that it can be explored and reflected on. But I have also written it because it is part of my story. I am a church planter with first-hand experience of planting a church that has gone on to plant churches that plant churches.[2] I have seen how it can revitalise the Church and its mission and see significant numbers of people responding to the love of Jesus Christ and seeing their lives beautifully turned around. And I am a bishop with a calling, and responsibility in the Church of England, to promote all kinds of church planting that includes resource churches. I have written this from a Church of England point of view (see endnotes for a simple glossary),[3] but I believe that much of the thinking, experiences and tools can be applied much more widely to any church that wants to plant or revitalise churches for the sake of the kingdom of God. Above all, I wrote this book because I believe that God is doing a new thing and that story is worth telling.

INTRODUCING RESOURCE CHURCH STORIES FROM ALL OVER ENGLAND

At the end of each chapter, I have invited a resource church leader to tell their story – how they got started, how they have planted or revitalised churches, and how they see their vision and mission worked out. I have also asked their respective bishops – mostly diocesans, but some area bishops too where appropriate – to comment on these resource churches under their oversight. I have chosen resource churches from around the country, in different contexts, and bishops from across the church traditions. There is still a way to go with broader diversity, but the resource church leaders I have chosen represent a snapshot of what exists right now.

The first story is from Alex Wood and Harbour Church. I chose this one not just because it's a good example of a resource church planted from scratch, but also because, at a personal level, they have just planted into the town where I was born and grew up – Gosport – which is particularly exciting for me. My hope is that as you read each chapter, and each of the stories and reflections from bishops, the pieces of the picture of the whole resource church in England picture will fall into place.

HARBOUR CHURCH PORTSMOUTH
Diocese of Portsmouth

> *Harbour Church Portsmouth began in September 2016 with just 20 people, and now welcomes 700 worshippers every Sunday to three different locations. It was planted from St Peter's Brighton and is part of the network run by Holy Trinity Brompton (HTB). It was designated as a resource church by the Diocese of Portsmouth as part of the diocese's strategy to create new worshipping communities over five years. Harbour Church has now in turn trained and sent a planting team to Cardiff.* **Alex Wood** *says:*

The creation of Harbour Church came about through a combination of our desire to plant a church similar to St Peter's Brighton (led by Archie Coates), and the diocese's own desire to create a church that would specifically appeal to students and young adults in the city of Portsmouth. The Archdeacon of Portsdown (the Rt Revd Dr Joanne Grenfell, now the Bishop of Stepney) approached Archie at the end of 2014 to see if St Peter's might be able to send a team to Portsmouth, and we were excited to be asked to lead this new plant. Having trained at HTB, I'd heard the vision of churches planting churches and

I've felt called to be part of this since my ordination. We were encouraged by Bishop Ric and others to look at joining the new wave of resource churches, and we were inspired by the new city-centre church at Gas Street Birmingham and others.

As we were all working on our vision for what might be possible, the emerging language of 'resource church' helped to frame our ecclesiology and to give us permission to move ahead, while helping us reassure and explain to the local clergy that we would be using a different model to a normal parish church, with the aim of having a city-wide impact.

We started working with the Bishop of Portsmouth (the Rt Revd Christopher Foster) in 2015 to find the most suitable location, and after exploring different options of church buildings in the diocese, we agreed we should move into commercial premises until the right property became available. In 2016, we planted with a team of 20 from St Peter's Brighton into a refurbished city-centre department store, and we were given a Bishop's Mission Order for Harbour Church and designated as a resource church by Bishop Christopher. In May 2016, I was also licensed as the Priest-in-Charge at St Alban's Copnor, a church in the east of the city that was vulnerable to closure. The congregation was graciously open to something radical and wanted to try something new, as the only alternative was to close!

By 2018, we were outgrowing the refurbished department store and needed more space, so we moved our Sunday congregations to St George's Portsea for our main morning services and started a new family afternoon service at St Alban's Copnor. It's been great to work together with the existing congregations at St George's Portsea and St Alban's Copnor, to help them to reach out to their local communities in new ways. We did not want to take over – we genuinely want to work in partnership with them. Our aim is to create one community, rather than two congregations sharing a building and worshipping separately. We similarly started evening services at All Saints Portsmouth in 2019, which attract a lot of students and young adults. We now have six services running across these three locations in the city.

We're also currently planting into Gosport, which is a smaller town within the diocese. I have recently become the interim Team Rector at Gosport and we're growing a team ministry there, as three parish churches have now become one parish. We're partnering with two of these small, existing congregations to create Harbour Church Gosport, and we'll be launching a new service in one of the buildings. The other remaining congregation will remain in its Anglo-Catholic tradition and we'll support and encourage what is already happening there. It can sometimes be a challenge for everyone to understand this new model of team ministry and leadership as it is so different, but these congregations have been identified as key areas for revitalisation so we're excited about all the possibilities. It's been great to be part of the Diocese of Portsmouth's strategy to inspire churches to grow in the depth of their discipleship, their impact in serving others, and in numbers of worshippers.

As I said in my first sermon at Harbour Church, we want this to be a place where people experience God's transforming love and show that love to others. When you are loved, you can love those around you. We often say that we are a church 'for the city' – we want to minister to the people of Portsmouth and make a difference in areas that need it most, working with those with addictions, the unemployed, the homeless, and those in debt. Since coming to Portsmouth, two particular issues have been prominent: poverty and food insecurity. This has spurred us to partner with King's Church Portsmouth and The Trussell Trust to launch a food bank, which worked throughout the pandemic. We've also started Harbour Coffee House, which aims to give job opportunities to the long-term unemployed, and we've begun a prison ministry, where we work with inmates to prevent reoffending and run chapel services and Alpha.

Two highlights stand out for me personally. Firstly, our City Women ministry, which aims to help vulnerable women in the inner city who might be involved in difficult family situations, have addictions, or have been sex workers. When we moved to Portsmouth we knew the statistics – the city has a disproportionally high number of women in the sex trade due to its naval history. It's a poor town economically and has a high rate of domestic abuse and gender-based violence.

We began to pray specifically for women in Portsmouth, and my wife Liz and others decided to run a spa morning and invite women. From that small beginning, we now work with all the domestic abuse refuges in the city, and we are their preferred supplier for support services and recovery. We also work with the British Red Cross to provide support for women suffering all sorts of abuse and trauma. We now have plans to set up a beauty spa room with a training centre for women coming out of sex trafficking to retrain and work in the spa.

Secondly, I love the recent story of a young man in his early 20s from Portsmouth who had never been in a church in his life. He met some young people from the church playing football one Wednesday evening, and came along with them the following Sunday to see what all the fuss was about. Soon, he left behind a life dominated by drugs and boredom, and found faith in Christ. Two weeks later, the country went into lockdown, and despite our fears his faith and reliance on God grew. He helped record and stream our online services, then did an internship, and is now considering full-time ministry. This has been a huge encouragement for us as we really want people to fall in love with Jesus and not our church.

We have always felt led to replicate our HTB roots by being a church that plants other churches. After launching the new worshipping community at St Alban's Copner, and then planting into St George's and All Saints, we had an opportunity to partner with HTB to plant a new church in Cardiff. In some ways, this has been very costly for us, as we sent Ryan Forey, our previous curate, and a team of 30 wonderful people to Cardiff, to start Citizen Church at St Teilo's Church. But it's been great to have this opportunity to start something new in the heart of this historic and significant city. The Bishop of Llandaff, the Rt Revd June Osborne, who invited Ryan and the team to plant Citizen Church, is clear that this plant is to be a church for the huge percentage of people who don't currently go to church. We're thrilled to be part of a planting story of four generations, from HTB to St Peter's Brighton, to Harbour Church, and now Citizen Church in Wales.

The Rt Revd Bishop Christopher Foster, Bishop of Portsmouth

The decision to designate a resource church in Portsmouth was fairly simple for me. The city of Portsmouth, with a population of less than a quarter of a million, is the second most densely populated city in the country after London. There are many young people, with over 20,000 students at the university alone. It was clear that the Christian Church in general, and the Church of England in particular, was only reaching a tiny number of those young people. Over the years, despite the faithfulness and energy of many, our existing parishes were making modest impact in that area, and this clearly needed addressing.

So, we turned to consider other approaches and looked 'down the coast' to the positive resource church experience at St Peter's Brighton. We opened a conversation about whether there might be a plant from Brighton into Portsmouth, and this ultimately came about through the generosity of St Peter's Brighton and the gift of wonderful leadership and the team of people who came from there to work with us.

We were confident in the vision for a resource church although the new is often, if not always, a challenge – some people were unsure, and wondered if they were being indirectly criticised, but they and we know the Christian Church and gospel is for everyone. There was no reason to be anything other than supportive, and people in the deanery and other churches welcomed the initiative, particularly when they saw people coming to know Jesus, engaged commitment to those marginalised in the community, and people learning about discipleship.

Our main challenge was premises and Harbour Church was launched on the upper floors of a former city-centre department store. In some ways, this was a good beginning, attracting publicity for not being 'church,' but it was expensive, incurring the costs for rent and to make fit for purpose as a temporary worship centre. It was a worthwhile investment though, and Harbour Church now has congregations and outreach from three different church buildings in different parishes in the city.

My initial aspirations and hopes for a resource church have been confirmed. Harbour Church has had an impact in reaching people with the good news of the kingdom who would not otherwise have been reached – it has grown, and its manifestations have been different across the city, with a ministry of outreach, service, and witness to particular disadvantaged or marginalised groups. This has had a significant impact on the city and it has helped us as a diocese to understand better how we might work collaboratively and resource each other in mission.

We wanted to continue the principle of supporting one another and to 'pass on' the model, in the same way that we in Portsmouth had benefitted and continue to benefit from the generosity of the St Peter's Brighton team. So, in the summer of 2020, when the call and the opportunity came in Cardiff to plant a church, it was a huge blessing to be able to work with Bishop June Osborne and for Harbour Church to gift a team to plant Citizen Church in Cardiff.

In addition to this new church, there have been many more encouragements throughout the process, particularly the generosity and commitment of the initial planting team, in their willingness to move to a new city, and in the way that Harbour Church has served and witnessed to the city of Portsmouth alongside other parishes and plants, reaching out to new people and drawing them into a life of faith, service, and new understanding.

CHAPTER 1

WHAT IS A RESOURCE CHURCH?

What do we really mean by resource churches? Many churches resource others in amazing ways but I want to be clear right from the start that we should regard a 'resource church' as something very specific. If defining it in one sentence, it would be this:

> *A resource church is designated by its bishop to be a church-planting church which trains leaders to resource and support mission across a diocese.*[4]

Five core elements describe resource churches:

1. Authorised by the diocesan bishop

The bishop, and the bishop only, can designate a church as a resource church because its calling and ministry goes beyond its own parochial boundaries. A resource church is invited and enabled to plant new churches and revitalise existing ones that lie in other parishes so that those churches can thrive in sharing the good news of Jesus to a world desperately in need of his love and grace. To do this canonically, it requires the authorising of a bishop. This sets resource churches apart from parish churches, not in a hierarchical sense, but as having a different vocation to parish churches, who have the responsibility and calling to reach their own parish. Resource churches are given a wider remit.

2. Part of a diocesan strategy to evangelise a city or town and transform society

Larger churches have traditionally been challenging to dioceses because their ministry often spills out beyond their parish boundaries. There has been no intermediate place for these churches between parish churches and cathedrals. The nearest equivalent historically are minster churches and Greater Churches, that often have larger clergy staffing, but these do not necessarily have larger memberships, nor a vision to grow the wider Church. Thus, larger churches have been contained within their boundaries and expected to contribute larger amounts to the Common Fund (or 'Parish Share')[5], since they have higher financial giving, without being encouraged to use the full range of their significant resources for wider mission.

Resource churches are recognised for the contribution they can make beyond the parish and, as such, can be used to play a significant part in the wider strategy of a diocese. Bishops and their senior teams can utilise their evangelistic and missional energy and resources to greater effect by directing them strategically to places of opportunity and need. This approach then enables dioceses to increase their vision and capacity and adds new pathways to respond to missional opportunities as they arise.

This marks a shift in the traditional relationship between bishop and parish church leader which, for good reason, has had an independence about it. A resource church leader becomes more of a colleague at diocesan level where they are able to offer new perspectives to strategic thinking and planning because they represent part of the wider strategic response. There is the opportunity to develop even more of a two-way, collegiate relationship. This is a considerable change to current culture and practice.

3. Intentionally resourced to plant and revitalise churches

Churches are communities of people who love God, who love their neighbours as themselves, and who love one another, where that love is so powerful that it is a deeply attractive community and a radically transforming community. This love is 'the greatest thing in the world'[6] and the greatest gift we can give. Sometimes our churches lose their way. For a whole host of reasons, some churches struggle, and others don't have the strength necessary to reach the people around them with the good news of the gospel. The church regularly needs renewal and revitalisation and, in some places, this is starting for the first time.

The church regularly needs renewal and revitalisation

Resource churches have the capacity to send teams made up from their members, led by leaders who are known and trusted by them, to plant new churches or revitalise existing churches. The creation of new Christian communities and the renewal and revitalisation of existing churches are some of the most interesting and exciting moves of God in England over the last 30 years. The Fresh Expressions movement has seen thousands of new churches with tens of thousands of members, including large numbers of people with no church background, connecting and growing as Christians. Pioneering has been recognised formally by the Church of England with the commissioning of pioneer ministers, both lay and ordained. Church revitalisations and church planting have been enabled as more and more bishops partner with church networks that offer to help in this way. We are seeing more and more networks actively planting churches within their parishes, or beyond with Bishop's Mission Orders (BMOs).

Resource churches have a vision to plant and revitalise churches. Dioceses can increase and accelerate their capacity to plant by directing existing resources, most vitally appointing curates to them, in order to revitalise or plant a church, in time, from that original resource church. In fact, you could say that a resource church is only really functioning as a resource church once it has actually planted its first church. Where new funding is available, or existing funds are redirected, this might be used to create the capacity to plant new churches out of the resource church. This kind of resourcing recognises that the investment made now will give a return in the future, in terms of new believers, stronger parishes, better maintained church buildings, and increased financial giving. Therefore, the intentional resourcing of resource churches increases this capacity to the benefit of the wider diocese.

A resource church is only really functioning as a resource church once it has actually planted its first church

4. Actively develops a pipeline of leaders for further planting

Churches that have been designated as resource churches are recognised as those which place a high value on the development of leaders within their congregations. This investment reaps a return in terms of the quality and quantity of lay leaders and an increasing number of vocations to ordained ministry. The vision of a resource church to plant, and their communication and strategy of that activity, means that leaders grow in a context where they see exciting opportunities to get involved themselves. In this way, resource churches are excellent environments for leaders to be formed for church planting, leading to a 'pipeline' of leaders being developed for deployment in future church plants. This is explored further in Chapter 8.

5. Provides other resources for mission across their city or town

Many churches are highly focused on developing their own discipleship and evangelistic capacity, using their own resources to deepen this work and make it more effective for their congregation in their context. Resource churches take these resources and add the dimension of giving them away to benefit the wider Church. This might include training courses in leadership, family life and relationship courses, evangelistic courses like the Alpha course,[7] running debt advice or food bank ministries.

Resource church leaders

It is worth saying something here about the specific calling and gifts of resource church leaders. It is one thing for a bishop to designate a church to be a resource church and to task it with the elements above. It is quite another thing to make it happen in practice. It needs a leader who is called and gifted, especially in leading a team on mission. An essential attribute of a resource church leader is to be apostolic, not in the Twelve Apostles sense, but in one that is about being sent to start new churches.

What I see in these leaders is that they call their churches to be audacious in seeking a vision bigger than themselves, generous in giving away leaders and people, humble in their attitude and practice, valuing unity in the church enough to seek its renewal and revitalisation, and they persevere in sending church planting teams year after year. While any church planter might have an apostolic calling, resource church leaders exercise it within a diocesan framework to do it again and again.

They call their churches to be audacious in seeking a vision bigger than themselves, generous in giving away leaders and people

The part that resource churches can play

A resource church then joins in with a diocese's mission to plant and revitalise churches in order to reach new people in new places in new ways. Its bishop appoints planting curates to them where they learn their trade before being sent to plant or revitalise other churches, taking a team and funding with them. Over time, those churches are renewed and begin to thrive, and that new mission energy impacts other churches so that the whole Church begins to grow. It is no surprise that some of the emerging leaders within them feel called to be ordained, and their only experience is of the church growing in number, depth and impact on the community.

Resource churches are called to play their part beyond the parish, generously offering their ministries and resources to the wider Church.[8] And because they behave in this way, resource churches can become ideal partners in strategic conversations with bishops and their senior staffs, knowing that these churches can be part of the solution to some of the challenges they face, reversing decline and seeing the Church grow again.

ST THOMAS' NEWCASTLE

Diocese of Newcastle

*St Thomas' is strategically located right in the heart of Newcastle and is surrounded by the two universities, retail, leisure, and transport. Its purpose is to see the many people who live, work, study, and play in the city, encounter the love of God. St Thomas' is entering an exciting new phase in its life as new congregations are planted and the church becomes a centre of mission, ministry, and church planting for Newcastle and the surrounding area. Designated as a resource church in 2019, it is part of the Diocese of Newcastle and is led by **Ben and Ellie Doolan**. Ben writes:*

Newcastle and the North East have a profound church planting heritage. Lindisfarne on Holy Island, in the Diocese of Newcastle, was sending out radical missionaries, evangelists, and church planters across the nation as early as the seventh century. In the medieval era, there were stories of many people encountering Jesus, being healed and baptised in Newcastle. Pilgrims began to flock to the city (and to this day there is a street in the city centre called Pilgrim Street). Many of these pilgrims were baptised as they encountered Jesus. This area of Newcastle became known as Jesus' mound, such was the impact of the gospel, and today this area of the city is known as Jesmond (a shortening of its original nickname). On their way to Jesmond through Newcastle, many of the pilgrims would be resourced and refreshed by a visit to St Thomas'.

St Thomas' has existed as a church family in Newcastle since the 12th century. In the 1820s, St Thomas' was impacted by a powerful move of the gospel. One plaque that still hangs in the church today describes the congregation as being 'few and unstable' but that it 'grew in spiritual strength' and that the influence of the church's ministry was soon felt far beyond the walls of the church. Historical records show that by the 1850s the average size of the congregation was just under 2,400, with 900 children and young people in church on Sundays. Another plaque in the church building refers to the new church building in the 1820s being built to help the church reach the many young people of the city. In other words, St Thomas' has a history of being a resource church in a region that has a history of sending church planters across this area and beyond.

In planting St Thomas' in October 2019, the church entered into a fresh phase of life as a resource church for the region and diocese. The church building is located right in the heart of the city, at the top of the main shopping street, by the civic centre, and is found right next door to both universities; the building is a city-centre landmark. Newcastle has one of the youngest age profiles of any city in the country, with the single biggest demographic being 20–24-year-olds, followed by 25–29s, then 15–19s, 30–34s, and then 0–4s. It is a young city. Bishop Christine quickly identified that St Thomas' would be the ideal location to begin to reach out to some of the age groups who live, work, study, or play in the city centre.

For several months after the launch, we saw young people make professions of faith every single week. Many of these were people who had no previous connection with the church before. We have seen students baptised, and the average age of our growing church family reflects the demographics of the city that we are called to serve. Our location is a dream for student ministry, with thousands of students walking past the church every single day. We have installed a wood-fired pizza oven outside the church and we regularly make fantastic pizza, give it away for free, and invite people to try church. This type of event and mission has led to many trying church for the first time and large numbers of guests on Alpha courses.

Just a few months after we launched, the Covid-19 pandemic struck, and through it God has done some amazing things. We launched our first small groups which, at the time of writing, have still been unable to meet in person, but they have been such a blessing as new people have joined the church through engaging with what we are doing online. Our youth worker has been taking a team of people to run detached youth work in Byker throughout the pandemic as he has been working with local church leaders in that part of the city. This has led to us planting a team in Byker which launched in summer 2021. We have hosted an online Alpha for the diocese and have had nine churches involved, each with their own breakout rooms for small groups. We have seen people coming to faith through the pandemic and have had a number of baptisms as a result of people checking out church online. It has felt like God has accelerated lots of things during the pandemic, despite its many challenges, frequent restriction changes, and unparalleled uncertainties.

The text on the plaque in the church that commemorates what God was doing at St Thomas' in the 1850s ends with a sense of prophetic hope by stating that the 'congregation dedicate this monument in the humble and fervent hope that an example so precious may be remembered and followed . . . in all time to come.' We believe this prayer of those faithful believers is being answered not just in Newcastle but around the country as new churches are planted. Bishop Christine often reminds our team of what God said to Isaiah:

'Forget the former things;
do not dwell on the past.
See, I am doing a new thing!
Now it springs up; do you not perceive it?
I am making a way in the wilderness
and streams in the wasteland.'

ISA. 43:18–19

We are claiming the promise that God is doing a new thing. He has done it before, he will do it again!

The Rt Revd Christine Hardman, Bishop of Newcastle

In Newcastle Diocese, we became interested in the concept of resource churches as a way of intentionally meeting the various needs of the many young people we have living in our city – there are 67,000 students at two tremendous universities, in addition to all the other young people in the city, and we could see that we were not really providing the kind of welcome and worship which would share the good news of Jesus with that age group. Of course, we see all of our churches as precious resources and they should all be resourcing others! But it's a useful shorthand to call them resource churches, although it may mean slightly different things in different dioceses.

It was important to us to have a type of church which does not just exist for itself but becomes a place of training for expertise to engage with a new people in a new way. Our diocesan vision is 'Growing Church Bringing Hope' and we developed a five-strand strategy to realise that vision. One major strand of our strategy was to establish a resource church in the city centre of Newcastle; a thriving church to meet the needs of the city. We focused on this for our Strategic Development Funding bid, in which we were greatly helped by Bishop Mark Tanner (then Bishop of Berwick). Bishop Mark was embedded in the New Wine network and helped us find the leader, Ben Doolan. St Michael le Belfry in York Diocese was officially the sending church, and at our invitation and delight, they sent 30 of their best team to Newcastle. We felt thrilled to be planted in and from the North of England.

Personally, I had no misgivings about resource churches, but I was well aware that some in other dioceses have felt resentful at the establishment of a new congregation receiving a lot of resource. I was aware that it might not be greeted with universal acclaim and I saw part of my task to help people not feel threatened by the emergence of something new.

At St Thomas', there was already a small congregation in place, with a completely different worshipping tradition. It also had a unique legal status, and was a separate charity, which caused some legal conundrums as the church did not have an incumbent but a Master, who had retired. With that vacancy, the wonderful location, and the supportive congregation, the chapel wardens and Archdeacon of Northumberland had the vision to say 'yes' to a new church, making St Thomas' their home. The whole vision came together in an extraordinary way. The existing congregation still meets in the mornings, and many are among Ben's biggest fans. The resource church meets at 4 p.m. on Sunday and it is encouraging to see the way God is working through the whole church, with much grace on all sides, not least from the existing congregation. There was a really outward-looking sense from them that things could not stay as they were, and they took a courageous step.

Before the process began, I had attended a seminar that Bishop Ric was leading. I was struck by the research and statistical analysis that showed the demographic of a place, and the specific conditions in which a resource church would best flourish. Looking at that data was important in our decision, as were the two most important success factors Bishop Ric identified – the high quality of the leader, which thankfully we have in Ben, and the 100 per cent backing of the diocesan bishop, to which I am fully committed.

In addition, the resource church should not be separate, but be strongly located as part of the diocese. Ben is deeply committed to the diocese in terms of ecclesiology and fellowship, and the church is entirely united in vision with others.

The team have done a very good job in creating such a welcoming and vibrant worshipping community. It was growing very well within just six months, and then lockdown happened in spring 2020, which was tough in the light of the effect it had on students and young people in particular. The church landscape changed overnight, and it was hard to keep up levels of energy and hope, but the team discovered all sorts of new ways that God was with us in the midst and they found grace in it all. None of us know what the future looks like, but we know that God is with us, and we all need the spiritual resources to not be overcome or disheartened with the journey.

My view on resource churches has not changed much during this process – I have long been of the view that we needed a new form of church in Newcastle Diocese, and I'm really encouraged by the way the church has fulfilled the hopes we've had for it from the beginning. It's what I would have hoped, the new kind of reaching out to that demographic. We are delighted with the results – the addition of a resource church enriches us as a diocese.

Resource churches fit well into the wider scope of the Church. Our pattern will be to have a resource church curate, and then what we are calling resourcing curates, who have a particular vocation to church planting (this may be starting a new congregation within an existing church) and a desire to invest in church growth in new ways. Those resourcing curates will be sent out, but linked back into the resource church for regular training and fellowship. The aim is that, funded by the diocese, St Thomas' will be a resourcing centre for expertise in church planting and growth, and other curates and incumbents will be connected back to the church for regular encouragement and training.

We are now looking for a resource church curate, and one of our challenges will be to develop a greater representation of women curates, which will in turn increase the number of leaders of resource churches who are women, particularly in larger charismatic evangelical churches which are predominantly male-led at present. We have some great women pioneers in Newcastle, and I am keen to encourage more diversity for women and people of BAME backgrounds – the more diverse we can be, the more we reflect what it means to be fully human.

RESOURCE CHURCHES – THE STORY SO FAR

Resource churches are being appointed at an increasing pace. In 2011, the term 'resource church' began being used of St Peter's Brighton to try to describe how a church like that could be a resource for mission to its diocese. There had been a few churches doing this already over the last few decades, but because it was done in such a focused way, over a short period of time, St Peter's Brighton marked something new. Since then, resource churches have been created year on year in the Church of England around the country (see figure 1) and there are plans at the time of writing for many more. By 2030, there may be as many as 300 resource churches of various kinds, playing their part in the renewal and reform of the Church in England.

By 2030, there may be as many as 300 resource churches of various kinds, playing their part in the renewal and reform of the Church in England

Total Resource Churches vs Year

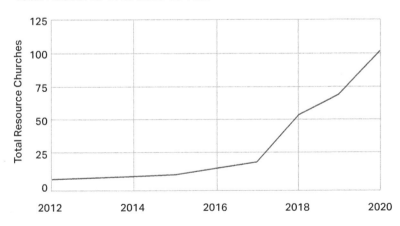

Figure 1. Number of churches designated as resource churches in England.

How resource churches have emerged

Three strands lie behind the resource church story in England:

1. Church attendance in English cities is lower than average. The Church of England's Strategy and Development Unit had started to map dioceses with local data showing that the Church of England was under-represented in cities, with lower church attendance and lower clergy resources per capita. Dioceses to date did not have a clear strategy to address this deficit with their own resources. An intervention was needed to see this change.

2. Holy Trinity Brompton (HTB) had started to plant churches beyond London. HTB's vicar, Nicky Gumbel, had begun to start using their church planting experience inside London, pioneered by former vicar, now Bishop Sandy Millar, and apply it further afield. After a successful plant at St Peter's Brighton, and in response to invitations from other bishops, they began to restructure themselves, allocating budgets and people resources, to meet the demand.

3. Bishop Richard Chartres, then Bishop of London, encouraged other bishops to explore planting partnerships with HTB. From 2011, Bishop Richard talked with other diocesan bishops about the idea of a church plant from outside their diocese to reach students and young people – one of the national Church's missing demographics – in their cities. He linked up interested bishops either directly with HTB or with me, in my role as his diocesan advisor for church planting at the time, and later as Bishop of Islington.

I believe that these three strands combined have led to the growth of resource churches across the country. Since these early beginnings, it has been a privilege for me to see the growth of these churches, their impact on local communities and the hopeful part they have to play in the future of the Church of England.

St Peter's Brighton

In 2009, the Bishop of Chichester invited HTB to reopen St Peter's Brighton by sending a new leader with a team of people. Archie Coates, who had been associate vicar at HTB, led a group of 30 people, who moved house, found new jobs and new places to live in and around Brighton. They cleaned and prepared the church and started new services there, particularly inviting people who had stopped going to church or who had never been to church to come along. The sacrifice of a planting team, combined with their enthusiasm, generosity and prayerfulness, is part of what makes a church plant unique, exciting and faith-making. That is attractive to those who come within its reach.

By 2017, they were recording a regular attendance of over a thousand people. Since they launched, they have gone on to revitalise six other churches, sending leaders and church members in teams to plant on to a local housing estate and another suburban church in Brighton, and churches in Hastings and Crawley, plus Portsmouth in another diocese, and to Bognor Regis in 2020 (see figure 2). Vitally, each of these plants or revitalised churches was enabled with the encouragement of their respective bishops.

Plants from St Peter's	Type and context	Place	Date
St Cuthman's Whitehawk	Estate church	Brighton	2013
Holy Trinity	Town centre church	Hastings	2014
Harbour Church	Resource church in another diocese	Portsmouth	2016
St John's	Town centre resource church	Crawley	2017
St Matthias Fiveways	Suburban church	Brighton	2017
St Wilfrid's	Town centre church	Bognor Regis	2020

Figure 2. Church planting from St Peter's Brighton since 2009.

Planting resource churches nationally

Before 2009, HTB had only planted or revitalised churches in London.[9] Following HTB's plant to Brighton, invitations from diocesan bishops began to be given, with plants to St Thomas Norwich, St Swithin's Lincoln and St Swithun's Bournemouth between 2013 and 2014. These teams were smaller but led by leaders who have become experts in managing change, sensitively navigating local nervousness, and building their membership through evangelism and effective discipleship.

By this stage, Mark Elsdon-Dew, communications director at HTB, was asked by Nicky Gumbel to explore opportunities for planting more resource churches by meeting with bishops who were making specific requests for them. Increasingly, Mark, representing HTB, and myself, in a more independent advisory role, would travel together to visit bishops and archdeacons to help diocesan teams to work out what it might look like for them. An acceleration of church planting began to happen nationally from HTB as ordained leaders were recruited and churches were planted to Gas Street Birmingham, Trinity Church Nottingham, St George's Gateshead, St Matthias Plymouth, St Werbergh's Derby, St Mark's Coventry, St Nicholas Bristol, Pattern Church Swindon, and St Mary's Southampton, all at the invitation of their respective diocesan bishops. Alongside this, with the support and encouragement of the New Wine network, St Philip's Salford was revitalised, as they began to explore the growing number of opportunities for resource churches to be created.

Sharing the story

In my capacity as the Bishop of London's advisor for church planting, I had already started to work on what a strategy for church planting might look like nationally. At the beginning of 2013, I found myself in a rather dingy, windowless, basement room to make a presentation that *There was a* was in stark contrast to the surroundings. I had been *palpable sense* invited by Bishop Richard to speak to a group of 50 *that something* bishops and diocesan secretaries, in Church House, *was afoot* Westminster, on how the Church of England might double in size in the coming years. There was a palpable sense that something was afoot. The first item on the agenda of that gathering was the establishing of 'city-centre resource churches':

> A key plank of a national church-planting strategy should be to plant large church-planting ('hub') churches in England's largest city-centres. Focusing on the cities – and thus influencing the large population centres – is a key way of reaching a whole nation . . . Over time, if suitably resourced, this church should be able to plant into the inner city and suburbs, and those churches should in turn plant into their adjacent areas.[10]

After several years of behind-the-scenes planning, praying, discussing and giving, these churches were created over the next few years, they have come to be called 'resource churches'[11] or 'resourcing churches.'[12] While the descriptor 'resource churches' is most commonly used, some dioceses have wanted to focus attention on the resourcing that they will do rather than the receiving of resources from the diocese. Bristol Diocese said of a resourcing church that 'its distinctive vocation is the deliberate resourcing of mission beyond its own congregation and location. It aims to grow and give away disciples and leaders by planting or strengthening other churches, developing ministers and providing other resources for mission.'[13]

Early central funding

In January 2014, the Spending Plans Task Group agreed to allocate up to £1M for the 'support and evaluation of new resourcing churches in urban conurbations (outside of London)' drawn from 'remaining Research and Development monies, which was agreed by the Archbishops' Council and Church Commissioners' Board.'[14] The analysis of church plants, which was undertaken as part of their church growth research, revealed the positive impact in terms of attendance growth and other factors (see figure 3). It showed an extraordinary reversal and counter-narrative to some of the measures of decline and deterioration seen elsewhere in the Church of England. The task group noted that 25 out of the 40 dioceses 'indicated that the likely trend in their diocese was an increase in the ministry being done through church plants' and they agreed to support the Dioceses of Birmingham, Lincoln, Manchester and Winchester with their current planting initiatives. They were also invited to consider the national picture, and discuss how best to encourage the development of resourcing churches across the country.

It showed an extraordinary reversal and counter-narrative to some of the measures of decline and deterioration seen elsewhere

Measure	Prior to plant	Postion now (in 2014)
Average congregation size	32	318
Average electoral roll	46	236
Average Parish Share paid	£16,500	£73,700
Typical state of the building	'Poor'	'Good'

Figure 3. The positive impact of revitalisation church plants, from church growth research undertaken by the Strategy and Development unit, National Church Institutions, 2014.[15]

Two years after that initial meeting, a gathering of bishops and diocesan secretaries met again in the same dingy basement rooms of Church House, Westminster, on 27 January 2015. This time, the Archbishop of Canterbury, Justin Welby, gave his support to the emerging resource church programme, sending a message saying, 'It would be great for every diocese to have a resource church – and not one, but two or three.'[16] It was a key moment of building confidence in the vision. It felt like a green light for the emerging work, and I noticed that the questions had changed more from 'why' to 'how.' The mood and tone were changing. This wasn't a maverick side show but was becoming mainstream. Following this, throughout the rest of 2015 and 2016, my work with individual bishops and dioceses began to increase significantly and I spent much time coaching them and working on their planting plans.

This growing momentum culminated with a gathering of 29 bishops, almost a third of the college, again invited by Bishop Richard Chartres, prior to the annual College of Bishops' meeting at St Hugh's College in September 2016. Against the background of church decline over decades, we told the story of six resource churches planted since 2009 and a further six planned for 2016 to 2017. That story was of remarkable 20-fold growth; from teams totalling 130 people to increased church attendance of 2,702; and of them going on to plant further churches, citing St Peter's Brighton and St Thomas Norwich which had between them planted seven churches in seven years. The early data being returned showed that 46 per cent of attendees were either new churchgoers or people returning to church after a long absence. It also showed that large numbers of young people were coming to newly planted resource churches with 30 per cent between 18 and 29 years old compared to the national average attendance of just 6 per cent in this age category in the Church of England (see figure 4).

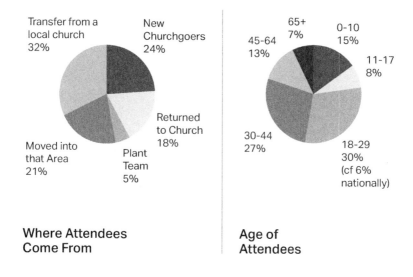

Where Attendees Come From

Age of Attendees

Figure 4. 2016 research based on a sample of six resource churches.

Sitting under long windows overlooking the serene gardens of St Hugh's College, we heard first-hand from Archie Coates and Tim Matthews, lead minister of St Swithun's Bournemouth.[17] They recounted extraordinary stories of growth, community impact and church planting, and we explored the lessons learned as to how resource churches could be created in dioceses. And as the bishops met over the next few days, many of my conversations focused on responding to invitations to give further consultations about resource churches around the country. Their reception was by no means unanimously welcomed, but the tide had turned from defending these plants and trying to persuade people of their merits, to responding to the growing momentum of questions and invitations.

Larger churches becoming resource churches

Early on in the thinking about creating resource churches was the recognition that there were many larger Anglican churches in cities already. What if they could be enabled and encouraged to plant and revitalise churches, to consider sending a planting curate with a team and funding? This would save all the time it took to identify a resource church leader, resource church location, or find the funding required to create the resource church in the first place, since it already existed.

The challenge that remained was whether an already existing larger church could create the capacity to plant, with the sacrificial costs of giving leaders, team and funding away, if it had not done so before; and whether they could work creatively and constructively with their bishop to plant beyond their parish. The mindset to 'give away your best' on a plant is hard to find as most churches do all they can to keep their members rather than give them away.[18] I remember Bishop Sandy Millar, then my incumbent in 2005, saying in our weekly meeting that 'if a church plant has not planted after five years, it might never plant, because it hasn't cultivated the DNA to do so.' And sometimes the relationship or history between bishop and incumbent of a larger church can hinder working in this way.

However, as resource churches began to be created, revitalising and planting other churches around them, many Anglican churches that had already had experience of church planting began to ask how they might become resource churches themselves. Bishops began to ask how they might play their part too in this programme. Interest and consultations with bishops and diocesan senior teams grew, and it was clear that something more formal was needed to ensure that all involved could learn from the growing body of experience that was emerging nationally.

Training to support practice

There were considerable obstacles to navigate in creating resource churches, both for bishops and their senior teams, and for the church planters themselves. I travelled the country, together with various colleagues and friends, delivering and developing training and consultancy sessions for bishops who had specifically asked for help in their dioceses[19] as they developed their own church-planting strategies. The number of greasy spoon cafés that served us along the thousands of miles of train journeys was directly proportional to the growth in the number of resource churches being created!

The training offered broadly covered four areas:

1. *Creating resource churches* – either from scratch or helping larger churches to become resource churches (see Chapter 6).

2. *Planting and revitalising churches* – from those resource churches as they prepared to plant, and helping them reflect and prepare to do it again (see Chapter 7).

3. *Developing leaders* – the recruiting, training, deployment and development of leaders both for leading and supporting church plants is critical to success (see Chapter 8).

4. *Developing diocesan church-planting strategies* – recognising that a multifaceted approach is both necessary and important to address the missional challenge of reaching the people in our dioceses with the gospel (see Chapter 5).[20]

These training sessions have played a vital part in supporting everyone involved in enabling these resource churches to get going in their contexts, where every single one is unique. Let me tell the story briefly of three dioceses, which were early adopters of resource church thinking and where I have been privileged to be involved in various ways. They serve as examples of how resources churches emerged within their diocesan strategies and practice.

Planting in and out of Birmingham

I met with Bishop David Urquhart in 2014 over a drink in Westminster to set out the opportunity of planting a resource church in Birmingham. A few months later he invited church leaders from the larger city-centre churches, Anglican and other denominations, to hear the vision for a city-centre resource church, particularly aimed at students, and geared towards resourcing the city, by planting and revitalising churches. It was a bold proposition that would impact every church in the city to some extent. I will never forget the moment when Mark Ryan, senior pastor of Birmingham City Church, said to Bishop David and all present, 'I think this is a great idea. I think it is of God. And we will give people and money to make it happen.' That generosity of spirit turned the meeting from information sharing to missional action. Following this, plans to plant a new resource church in the parish of St Luke's Birmingham were formed and passed through the diocesan governing structures. Tim and Rachel Hughes[21] were invited to lead a team from HTB to plant a church in the nightclub quarter of the city around Broad Street. In September 2015, 30 people moved up to Birmingham with Tim and Rachel, meeting in various venues before settling in the Retort House on Gas Street, which was bought and developed through various grants and a loan to the new church's PCC. It came to be called Gas Street Church.

Within their first year, they had planted their first church, another resource church led by Phil and Rachel Atkinson, located in Coventry. Gas Street had been working with the diocesan team to identify locations in Birmingham in which to plant, but they experienced the challenge of matching people with opportunities. Meanwhile, the church continued to grow to beyond 700 in its first three years. This prompted the diocese to work more closely with them and other churches wanting to join in with planting, culminating in a diocesan church-planting strategy in September 2018. This included a goal to start 100 new worshipping communities by 2028. 'Most of these would be small fresh expressions of church but some would be full-scale church plants, with a team and leader being sent from one church to form or revitalise another, using a four-phase approach to help planting become "normal" in every deanery.'[22]

Planting resource churches in Winchester Diocese

Meanwhile, the Bishop of Winchester, Tim Dakin, invited HTB to send a planting curate to plant into the closed St Swithun's Church in Bournemouth town centre. Data had shown that this area was, along with Poole, one of the larger urban areas of the country with a significant student population who were not being seen in local churches. Tim and Debi Matthews came with a team of 10 from London and launched the plant in September 2014. The church grew quickly with informal Sunday services, Alpha and relationship courses, and they opened a homeless shelter to begin to help those caught in addictions. Two and a half years later, St Swithun's joined with St Clement's Boscombe to revitalise the church and work with its two church schools, extending their mission to that area.

In September 2018, Jon and Hannah Finch were invited to revitalise St Mary's Southampton by the Bishop of Southampton. The church has grown significantly, reaching students and young adults in Southampton city centre. In 2021, they are planting into nearby Totton and taking responsibility for a neighbouring church. Six months after the Finches arrived in Southampton, Chris Bradish was installed as the new vicar to revitalise St Mary's Andover by the Bishop of Basingstoke, David Williams. All these church revitalisations were part of a joined-up strategy by the Diocese of Winchester and were trained, planted and supported by HTB. In 2019, the diocese began conversations with three other existing larger churches in the diocese to become resource churches, connecting them all together to form a single learning community.

Complementing Fresh Expressions in Leicester Diocese

Within the overall aim of creating 320 Fresh Expressions of church in their diocesan strategy,[23] Bishop Martyn Snow appointed six Leicestershire churches, or teams of churches, as resourcing churches in July 2018. They were The Cornerstone Team, Holy Trinity Leicester, The Harborough Anglican Team, Emmanuel Loughborough (working in partnership with the Good Shepherd Church), St John's Clarendon Park and St John's Hinckley. They were to complement the overall mission strategy to reach the 93 per cent of people who were not currently part of any Christian community in their diocese. Their stated hope and aim were for the resourcing churches to double in size over the next 12 years, and each to plant six new worshipping communities over the next six years, with a range of diverse models of church to reach different groups of people. They described how some would be small 'grass roots up fresh expressions of church, starting with just two or three people.' Others would be larger plants and revitalisations with a planting curate and teams of 20 or so people.[24]

We can see from these three examples how dioceses differed in their strategy and methods, but it was exciting to see momentum for resource churches was rapidly growing.

A growing momentum

The number of resource churches continued to grow consistently after 2009 and passed the 100 mark by the end of 2020. The number jumped quickly in 2017 with the appointment of 19 resource churches in London Diocese.[25]

It is not just in cities. Resource churches are being created in market towns and rural areas too

Other dioceses have also appointed larger numbers of resource churches as they saw their potential. It is not just in cities. Resource churches are being created in market towns and rural areas too. Southwell and Nottingham, for example, have a goal of creating 25 resource churches alongside their desire to plant 75 new worshipping communities, including in towns and villages.[26] But this is more than just numbers. The development of resource churches nationally is happening in many ways.

Growth in this area has been greatly assisted by an increase in training, enabling resource churches to be created and then helped to plant again and revitalise churches. There are now cohorts of resource church leaders at different stages of development being trained and supported in their work, while individual support for bishops and their teams is happening across the country. Diocesan mission directors are being drawn together not only to

Diocesan mission directors are being drawn together not only to learn from each other about resource churches but to share wider missional strategies

learn from each other about resource churches but to share wider missional strategies. And church networks like the Church Revitalisation Trust (formed to support HTB's planting work) and New Wine are supporting resource church leaders and church planters, together with emerging Anglo-Catholic networks. In London, where we appointed resource churches across different church traditions, I have led learning communities for them to develop their planting plans in ways that affirm their traditions and enable them to learn from each other. Even if it feels a bit like treading on glass sometimes, there are so few cross-tradition opportunities for learning that the effort is important and worthwhile.

Funding from the central church has been a significant factor in helping dioceses to push through the inertia of starting something new. From the first £1M grant for resource churches in 2013, dioceses have applied for funds from the Strategic Development Funding (SDF) to support a range of initiatives, including creating resource churches. This has come in different ways for different projects. Funds have gone towards resource church staff, building development, training and support costs, depending on each individual situation. In each case, dioceses have to add their own funds to match the SDF grants and they are held to close scrutiny of outcomes so that there is appropriate accountability. This has at times been controversial, as other sectors of the church have appealed for funds too, sometimes successfully, sometimes not. What I have seen, as I have consulted with individual dioceses, is that many of them recognise that spreading funding thinly across the board, so everyone gets the same, does not lead to the changes that are necessary to see development and growth. A strategic, more targeted, approach is necessary to use valuable funds in ways that produce tangible results.

As the journey proceeded, it became clear that the church planting movement needed additional support and oversight that could not be solely provided by the dioceses, church commissioners, or by individual churches or networks. In earlier conversations with Bishop Richard Chartres, it became clear that a centre for church planting and church growth should form a helpful focus for encouraging and developing the work. This became a reality when he asked me to become the Bishop of Islington, to oversee church planting in the London Diocese and to offer national and more formal support to all dioceses. We created the Gregory Centre for Church Multiplication, funded by various trusts and project grants, focused on supporting the Church to reach those who are not yet connected with it. A part of the Centre's work is to provide structured support for resource churches in various ways, including online courses, teaching resources, webinars and conferences, including one in 2020 attended by over 200 resource church leaders, planting curates and resource church operations managers.

Changing England's cities

The growth of resource churches has been an extraordinary story in the life of the Church of England in recent years. It has met a need to revitalise churches where our denomination is in decline and it has stirred up new vision and energy alongside some of the other exciting missional movements in the Church in recent years. But it is also a movement in its infancy and there are many challenges and criticisms that have been raised that are good for its formation – I address some of the criticisms in Chapter 9 and there is a short section on how resource churches have responded to the coronavirus pandemic in Chapter 10. I am personally very excited by all that resource churches are doing in the Church of England. They are not a silver bullet or the only solution to what the Church is facing, but they are playing an important part in changing England's cities and their story deserves to be told.

FOUNTAINS CHURCH BRADFORD

Diocese of Leeds

Fountains Church was commissioned by the Bishop of Bradford, the Rt Revd Dr Toby Howarth, in September 2019. It will be based in Bradford's regenerated City Park, and its vision is to be a fountain of living water to bless the city. It is led by **Linda Maslen***, who writes:*

Fountains Church was launched as an afternoon service in September 2019 with around 150 people attending and a commissioning by the Bishop of Bradford, the Rt Revd Dr Toby Howarth. It's not a comfortable church – we have a vision to be a sending and resourcing church from the very beginning, to grow and send out leaders to bless the city. In time, our physical home will be a former city-centre nightclub, but we will be on the move from the start. Even as we are setting off, our heart is to find those whom we can send.

Our vision is to love God, live as family, and be fountains of living water to bless Bradford. The church's name is drawn from its future location: by next year the congregation will move to our new building overlooking the City Park fountains of Bradford. It's a well-loved area of the city, with the fountains creating a relaxed, continental feeling, and we hope this will be a space where we can build relationships and share Jesus. The ground floor of our new venue (previously three different nightclubs) will be converted into a 250-seat auditorium and café. The next phase will involve remodelling the first floor to create an 800-seat auditorium overlooking the city, the fountains, and Bradford's City Hall.

The team was excited to discover that two congregational churches previously existed on the site – the first in the 18th century was knocked down to build a larger 800-seater in 1861, called the Cathedral of the Non-Conformists, with services led by preachers such as Titus Salt and Jonathan Glyde. The vision of these worshippers was that there would be nothing lacking for the expansion of religious and spiritual growth in Bradford; and Fountains Church is passionate about reclaiming this legacy and seeing God's kingdom grow in its fullness across the city. The church is supported by the Diocese of Leeds and New Wine, both of which have a vision to see local churches impacting communities with the love of God.

The team is passionate about reaching different demographics in Bradford, including students at the nearby university and college, those working and visiting the magistrates' court, businesses in the city, and those on the margins of society. We may have a service based around wrestling, with a boxing ring in the church, to draw in young people who are struggling, particularly drawn from the Asian community in the city. We are also looking at holding exercise classes during the week, creating relationships with those in the area who wouldn't usually attend a church.

The worshipping community that is forming is eclectic, coming from Bradford and beyond. Around 25 people served as team members at the launch, including four members who have moved to the city to be part of this new venture. Being a resource church led by a woman also lends a different dynamic to the team and it's great that I am part of a small group of women leading and growing larger churches, as we can bring something different to the equation. Hopefully I can be an encouraging example for those following in my footsteps. I was born in Bradford and gave my life to Jesus in 1977 at St George's Hall in the city. I felt God calling me back to Bradford when the prospect to lead Fountains Church suddenly appeared, and I still feel both excited and daunted by the task. It seems impossible without God, but when I put God back at the centre and see the need in the city, it feels an amazing opportunity to serve my hometown.

Leadership has to be about developing future leaders. Growing others is one of the ways we best grow ourselves as leaders. My background in business, which included heading up call centres for HMRC, also informs my passion to grow leaders and a desire to send others out. The team is excited about developing missional communities in the workplace. We can't just plant with clergy – we need lay people to start different types of ministries such as worshipping communities at work. We also hope to develop lay leaders in our congregation who can start missional communities in some of the areas surrounding Bradford. Leadership is about identifying those behind us and preparing others to lead from the outset, whether it's in the workplace or leading different churches in the future.

This, along with mentoring and discipling people well, is to be the hallmark as the community develops. The aim is to see people come to church to see us one Sunday and to encourage them to be serving on team the next. We are also keen to encourage those who are members of other churches to maybe come along occasionally, not to move to Fountains, but perhaps to experience a different kind of worship while continuing to serve week by week in their own, often smaller, churches.

I am also the regional director for New Wine, covering the North East and Yorkshire, and this is another way in which Fountains is able to resource others. We have been hosting monthly New Wine celebrations and round tables and mentoring groups that encourage and help develop and support other church leaders.

As Fountains came to the end of its first year of worship in 2020, the first stage of the building renovation was nearly complete, giving a worship and community space that will accommodate 200 people and a café that will hold

100 more. The team worked alongside others during the period of the Covid-19 pandemic and are creating social enterprises that will support those who are affected either economically, socially, or physically by the after-effects. The team at Fountains know there will be many challenges ahead as we join in with what God is doing in Bradford, but we know that through all things God will be faithful and we are excited for all that is to come.

The Rt Revd Dr Toby Howarth, Bishop of Bradford

Ever since arriving in Bradford as bishop in 2014, I had heard people talk about planting a church in the city centre. The conversation normally ended with, 'It probably wouldn't work here; this is Bradford.'

The atmosphere, however, was changing and the city centre architecture was a big part of that change. From a vast building site 'hole,' for example, that I had seen on earlier visits, emerged a shiny new shopping centre. Along with work on other historic buildings, it felt as though there was a renewal of hope and self-confidence in the city as a whole.

So, when Bishop Ric encouraged some of us Anglican church leaders to think about putting in a bid for a new resource church in Bradford, we wondered if the time was now right. In the end, after prayer, consultation, and heart-warming support particularly from existing churches, we put in a bid for Strategic Development Funding. We proposed a three-stranded approach: building a network of small missional communities for our hard-pressed inner-city and outer-estate parishes; bringing together, strengthening, and challenging a network of five resourcing churches across the Bradford district; and planting a new resource church in the city centre.

We were disappointingly knocked back on the small missional communities, but successful with the other two parts of the bid. We knew, whatever models were being tried out elsewhere, that the resource church had to be truly 'Bradford.' That meant young, entrepreneurial, and diverse. It meant the church investing into the city's vision of renewal, growth, and well-being, with an offer of the abundant life that God offers to us in Jesus.

This offer has particular challenges in a place like Bradford and in a post-Covid world. The city centre is one of the few places in Bradford which belongs to everyone: the fountains in summer see an extraordinary mix of families playing, chatting, and laughing together. The name 'Fountains Church' calls to mind both the literal water-jets in City Park and the living water Jesus offers. Our new church affirms the diversity of the city while calling people to follow Christ.

The future of city centres felt different after months of virus-induced lockdown. Retail and office working was hit hard. Covid revealed and exacerbated existing health and economic inequalities which are all too evident among the marginalised people who frequent City Park. Fountains Church sits in the middle of these challenges, with a stake in the future of the city centre. We are a diverse body of people, and we reached out, throughout lockdown, as much to those on the edges as to young professionals, both socially distanced where possible and online. New social enterprises focused on the provision of affordable, intercepted food.

Bradford's churches are in a time of rapid and unsettling change. Fountains Church, as a resource church, along with our network of what we are calling 'resourcing churches,' is a welcome part of this new ecology. Fountains Church has already planted a new congregation among those struggling with challenges such as addiction. There are exciting possibilities now for revitalisation and planting more widely in Bradford. We are grateful and hopeful.

CHAPTER 3

THE THEOLOGY UNDERPINNING RESOURCE CHURCHES

Resource churches today find their biblical roots in the great sending churches of the early church. The churches in Jerusalem, in Antioch and in Ephesus played a significant part in the evangelisation of their regions and in setting a framework for church growth and church planting. How were they created? How did they develop and grow?

Jerusalem

The church in Jerusalem was the first church.

Its hallmark was constant prayer and the infilling of the Holy Spirit. As they were praying at Pentecost, they were filled with the Spirit and empowered to be witnesses. As the church grew, the new believers devoted themselves to prayer, and when they were banned from talking about Jesus by the Sanhedrin, they prayed for boldness in speaking about Jesus and for signs and wonders to be performed. It is as the church prays that it receives the Spirit.[27]

Its leadership was apostolic. Of course, the first leaders were the apostles, but they sent out many apostolic leaders like Philip and Barnabas across the region to evangelise, preach and heal the sick. They developed a pipeline of missionally minded, servant-hearted, culturally diverse leaders who were appointed as deacons in serving roles as well as going out to preach the gospel.

They developed a pipeline of missionally minded, servant-hearted, culturally diverse leaders

It was 'launched' at Pentecost at a moment of maximum impact on a broad international stage which set the church up for multiplication. Thousands of visitors from all over the known world were worshipping at this important Jewish festival. They went home carrying the message about following Jesus, the Lord and Messiah who had risen from the dead, and receiving the gift of the Holy Spirit. The church also enjoyed the favour of local people. As the apostles performed signs and wonders, huge crowds came from surrounding towns and villages, bringing the sick and demonised, and they were all healed. It behaved as an attractional church, drawing from a wide area around the city.

Its practices had four core elements that characterised Christian gatherings in the early church.[28] They devoted themselves to the apostles' teaching – Peter, John, Stephen and Philip all quote extensively from the Scriptures as they evangelise and teach others; to fellowship, meeting in public places and in their homes, sharing everything in common with huge generosity and care for one another; to the breaking of bread, reminding themselves about Jesus' words at the Last Supper, and sharing meals together with glad and sincere hearts; and to prayer, both intercession and prayer for healing and miracles.

It was an evangelistic church as the apostles and other disciples took every opportunity to witness about Jesus. Peter spoke to the crowds at Pentecost calling them to 'repent and be baptised . . . in the name of Jesus Christ for the forgiveness of your sins' (Acts 2:38) and there was a huge response. Peter and John told the Sanhedrin that they could not help speaking about what they had seen and heard. Stephen spoke boldly to the high priest and the Sanhedrin about Jesus from the Old Testament. Evangelism was at the heart of the practice of this church. And as a result, the church grew rapidly with thousands joining the church, including Hellenistic Jews and Hebraic Jews and large numbers of priests.

It faced opposition from the authorities who were threatened and filled with jealousy. They arrested leaders, hoping to quell the growth of the church. They treated them unfairly and unjustly, calling on false witnesses and punishing them without charge. The danger of the threat of arrest was matched by miraculous escapes from prison. Peter and John were flogged by the Sanhedrin for preaching, yet they left 'rejoicing because they had been counted worthy of suffering disgrace for the Name' (Acts 5:41). This only served to increase their resolve. A great persecution broke out after the martyrdom of Stephen, scattering its members throughout Judea and Samaria.

It became an apostolic mission base, as the apostles went on evangelistic trips and church-planting missions to the neighbouring regions. Philip preached in Samaria and was joined by Peter and John where they experienced a huge response visiting other villages on the way back to Jerusalem. Philip led an Ethiopian eunuch to the Lord in the desert before going to Azotus and all the way on to Caesarea. Peter visited believers in Lydda and Sharon and saw the whole towns turning to the Lord after a dramatic healing. Another healing, of Tabitha in Joppa, led to many people turning to the Lord. Peter also visited Caesarea to preach to Cornelius the centurion's household, seeing Gentiles turning to Christ.

What a model for resource churches today!

Antioch

The church in Antioch was a multicultural, missionary church, resourcing church planting in the regions and nations around the known world.

It was established as persecuted Christians, originally from Cyprus and Cyrene, were scattered as far as Antioch, 500 miles north of Jerusalem. They proclaimed the gospel about Jesus to Hellenists there and large numbers became Christians. This cross-cultural mission and evangelism led to new groups of people coming to faith in Jesus and the church in Antioch emerged as a bicultural church, with Jewish and Gentile converts. News of this reached the church in Jerusalem and they sent Barnabas to discover what was happening there. Barnabas, himself from Cyprus and who might have known some of the original Antiochene evangelists, was delighted with their faith and encouraged them to remain faithful. He then went to find the newly converted Saul, brought him back to Antioch, and together they spent a year teaching large numbers of people. They deepened their identity in Christ, becoming known as 'Christians,' welcomed prophets from Jerusalem, gave generously to the famine-struck church in Jerusalem, and developed leaders with prophetic and teaching gifts.

As it grew, the church in Antioch discovered a new calling to send missionaries and plant churches. Its leadership team heard the Holy Spirit telling them, as they prayed, to 'set apart for me Barnabas and Saul for the work to which I have called them' (Acts 13:2). The outcome was the first mission journey to Cyprus and Galatia, where the gospel was preached in new countries, people from diverse backgrounds came to faith in Jesus and new churches were planted. They continued to send Paul and Barnabas and others out and welcomed them back.

The attributes of Antioch as a 'resource church' were numerous:

- It was led by a multicultural, multinational and multi-gifted leadership team that must have contributed to its outward-facing vision and readiness to send its leaders on mission.

- It strengthened its members with high-quality teaching ministry from Barnabas and Saul, who developed many others to teach and preach as well, as well as a powerful prophetic ministry in its senior leadership team.

- It sent missionary leaders who planted churches that multiplied across regions, starting with familiar places and then going further and further afield.

- It managed leadership conflicts by commending both Paul and Barnabas after they fell out with each other, with an outcome of two trips not just one.

- It celebrated mission trips on their return as the church gathered to hear stories of God at work.

- It became a centre for missionary learning as Paul developed his strategies each time he returned, developing his team size and roles on the second journey, and applying the principle of multiplication on the third in Ephesus.

- It stayed connected with the church in Jerusalem as they welcomed decisions about circumcision and received prophets Agabus, Judas and Silas with an enthusiastic welcome. They regarded the church of Jerusalem as senior to them without any sense of competition or malice in spite of their differences.

The church at Antioch was distinct from the church in Jerusalem in its sending of missionaries and church planters further afield, developing links with churches all over the known world as leaders came back and forth, and as a result being very international and intercultural. For the Gentile mission, this was the preferred home base for Paul the apostle.

Ephesus

The church in Ephesus made a massive impact on a whole region in just a few years through the training and multiplication of indigenous church planters.

Paul had this strategic, regional city in his sights during his second mission journey, but the Holy Spirit kept him from preaching in that province.[29] It was home to the Temple of Artemis, one of the seven wonders of the ancient world, which physically and culturally dominated the city.[30] Paul managed to make a fleeting visit on his way back from Corinth to Antioch. He briefly visited the synagogue there and tantalisingly said, 'I will come back if it is God's will'.[31]

Sometime later, Paul did return and found a group of twelve men who he led to Christ, baptised them and then prayed for them. They were filled with the Holy Spirit, spoke in tongues and prophesied. He spent three months in the synagogue speaking boldly and arguing persuasively about the kingdom of God. The message was not wholeheartedly received and some of those listening raised objections and spoke up publicly against Paul's teaching. Rather than outstay his welcome, Paul moved to a more neutral venue called the hall of Tyrannus where he hosted daily discussions. We read next that, 'This went on for two years, so that all the Jews and Greeks who lived in the province of Asia heard the word of the Lord' (Acts 19:10).

Paul does not appear to have left Ephesus during that time, devoting himself to debating, persuading, teaching and training disciples daily in the hall of Tyrannus and going from house to house preaching and building up the churches that met there and warning them 'night and day with tears' (Acts 20:31). Yet, the whole province heard the word of the Lord. How was this remarkable feat achieved? It seems that Paul was not just training disciples, but also church planters.

It seems that Paul was not just training disciples, but also church planters

When Paul wrote to the Colossians, he said that he had never visited the city (Col. 2:1). It was Epaphras, who went on Paul's behalf (1:7), who first told them about Jesus and established a church there. It seems he might also have planted the churches in Laodicea and in Hierapolis (4:13) which were very close geographically.[32] Epaphras was from Colossae (4:12). Neil Cole conjectures that Epaphras perhaps travelled to Ephesus on business, was converted, discipled and trained by Paul, before being sent back to his home town to plant new churches.[33] Whether this was what happened or not, the church planting of Epaphras, as one of perhaps many church planters sent out from Ephesus, gives an insight into how the whole province of Asia heard the word of the Lord.

Ephesus was one of the seven churches written to in the book of Revelation and it seems likely that they were planted during this time as well. The churches written to were in Ephesus, Smyrna, Pergamum, Thyatira, Sardis, Philadelphia and Laodicea and they follow an oval shape of cities around the inside of the province of Asia. In addition to the churches in Colossae and Hierapolis, we know there was also a church in Troas, on the northern sea-border of Asia, that Paul went on to visit. These churches in these cities alone represent quite a spread of mission activity, and in all likelihood, they might also have planted into the towns and villages around them. All Asia had heard the word of the Lord from church planters like Epaphras who had planted churches, that planted churches, that planted churches throughout the region. Multiplying church planting was in the very DNA of the church at Ephesus.

Multiplying church planting was in the very DNA of the church at Ephesus

Like Jerusalem and Antioch, supernatural signs and wonders were part of church life in Ephesus. God did extraordinary miracles through Paul with many sick and demonised people being healed. Magic, superstition and spiritual practices were common in the city, probably connected to the worship cult of Artemis there. Paul, in his letter to the Ephesians, writes to them about the need to 'put on the full armour of God so that you can take your stand against the devil's schemes' (Eph. 6:11). Through these spiritual battles the church in Ephesus made a massive impact on the social fabric of the city. New believers confessed their sins publicly and burned sorcery scrolls valued at more than £3M in today's currencies. The local economy was massively impacted by the gospel that was changing people's buying habits. Local business leaders rioted in response, requiring the city magistrates to get involved, who were clear that Paul had honoured the local culture, which showed the depth of feeling towards the growing influence of the church there.[34]

The church in Ephesus had grown to impact the whole city, drawing large numbers of new believers and changing the local economy and the spiritual atmosphere. Local citizens held the name of Jesus in awe. Through Paul's leadership, the church had sent church planters to start new churches in major cities, towns and villages such that the whole province, both Jews and Greeks, had heard the word of the Lord. What sets this church apart is that Paul planted the first church in Ephesus. All the others were planted by other people.[35] Cole attributes the success of this mission to Paul selecting Ephesus as a strategic base camp, where he increased his spiritual and relational authority, constantly mentoring individuals one-to-one and raising up leaders who had a huge impact everywhere else. There is no question that the church in Ephesus influenced the whole region. It resourced mission for its city, and for the whole of Asia, sending out church planters to its cities, towns and villages, so that many heard and responded to the gospel of Jesus Christ.

Theological foundations

Jerusalem, Antioch and Ephesus are inspiring and informing examples of what resource churches could be in today's church. What about the theological foundations of the five core elements of resource churches?

Authorised by a bishop

Authority is required to appoint people into positions of authority.

From the earliest years of the church, apostles and overseers were involved in appointing church planters and elders. Resource churches plant churches and revitalise Church of England parishes. So, when a parish is planted into or revitalised, it must be with the bishop's authorisation, because the bishop exercises spiritual and legal authority over that parish in their diocese. Ordaining and sending

Ordaining and sending out ministers is a crucial part of episcopal ministry

out ministers is a crucial part of episcopal ministry where 'they are incorporated within the historic ministry of the church in continuity with the mission of the apostles, as a tangible sign that it is the same church.'[36] Bishops are therefore vital in this commissioning work.

The House of Bishops endorsed church planting in general and resource churches in particular in their June 2018 statement, 'Church Planting and the Mission of the Church':

> Church plants that aspire to be resource churches (church-planting churches supporting a wider area) will have a clear strategy for developing as resource churches for the surrounding area, and/or for further planting into other places. This will be built into the planning and consultation with other neighbouring church communities from the start, with the resourcing (including clergy and lay leaders) planned accordingly. The bishop's leadership role is key in supporting this planning.[37]

Part of a diocesan strategy to evangelise a city or town and transform society

Why should a diocese have a strategy and what part should a resource church play in it?

The Church of England's understanding of its mission is summarised in the 'Five Marks of Mission':[38]

1. To proclaim the Good News of the Kingdom.

2. To teach, baptise and nurture new believers.

3. To respond to human need by loving service.

4. To seek to transform unjust structures of society, to challenge violence of every kind and to pursue peace and reconciliation.

5. To strive to safeguard the integrity of creation and sustain and renew the life of the earth.

Furthermore, the Church of England describes itself as 'a Christian Presence in Every Community.'[39] This is like the church's vision statement. These outward-facing marks and this vision statement are a continual challenge to us because we fall far short. When Bishop Newbigin returned from ministry in India in 1985, he was taken aback by the secularisation of England and Western Europe. He said, 'If one looks at the world scene from a missionary point of view, surely the most striking fact is that, while in great areas of Asia and Africa the church is growing, often growing rapidly, in the lands which were once called Christendom it is in decline.'[40] This decline has been our reality for decades despite Jesus' call for us to be missionary by nature. We need a transformation to become the pilgrim people of God who are called to present the gospel in a complex modern world.[41]

The 2004 *Mission-shaped Church* report picks this up. 'We believe the Church of England is facing a great moment of missionary opportunity.'[42] To meet this opportunity, a plan is needed. A strategy is simply a plan of action designed to achieve an overall aim. In a diocese this will be multifaceted. Helping parishes to engage with this mission is the work of any bishop[43] and church planting is a part of this.[44]

The Church of England parochial system has been an essential and central part of the national church's strategy to deliver incarnational mission to every person in the country. But there is an increasing body of opinion that says the existing parish system alone is no longer fully able to deliver its underlying mission purpose. A variety of integrated missionary approaches is required. We need a mixed ecology of parish churches and network churches, including 'fresh expressions of church,' in an active partnership across a wider area, because the 'diverse consumer culture will never be reached by one standard form of church.'[45]

We need a mixed ecology of parish churches and network churches

Reversing decline means seeking growth. Jesus pointed towards this growth as he taught parables about the kingdom of God. When the gospel is preached there should be an expectation of growth in many dimensions – in depth of commitment and discipleship, in being faithful and being present and in number with more people responding.[46] We need to recover the apostolic DNA of the early church so that the gospel can be communicated afresh in this generation and the church can grow again.

One of the great encouragements for the church is that God is already at work. He is on mission and invites us to join in with him. The *missio Dei* means that God is always taking the initiative and we can experience the joy of discovering that he has gone before us. And that changes our perspective. Chris Wright expressed it by saying, 'It is not so much that God has a mission for his Church in the world, but that God has a Church for his mission in the world.'[47] So as we plant new churches, in places, reaching new people, we are enacting this mission and he grows the Church around us.

But a mindset of growth alone is inadequate. The Scriptures point towards multiplication as a way that growth can happen, leading to more prolific results. The multiplication of churches should be normal.[48] Some have gone further to say that if there is no reproduction of churches, then that church is sterile.[49] In our own mission context, we need to recover the natural and emerging instinct of the early church which was to reproduce itself.[50] This is achieved at a local level, by adopting a sending approach to growing the church. This has the potential to lead to new churches being created.[51] Thus, the planting and multiplication of churches plays its part in growing the Church.

Intentionally resourced to plant or revitalise churches

Church planting describes the ministry of creating new churches. Paul said, 'I planted the seed, Apollos watered it, but God has been making it grow' (1 Cor. 3:6). Watering might be said to describe teaching and strengthening existing churches, following Apollos' well-appreciated teaching ministry (Acts 18:24–28). Planting churches is primarily a spiritual activity where Jesus is the 'real church planter,' building his Church and growing it by adding new believers, opening hearts, and increasing, spreading and multiplying the Word of God.[52]

Jesus is the 'real church planter,' building his Church and growing it by adding new believers, opening hearts, and increasing, spreading and multiplying the Word of God

Even though the activity of church planting is as old as the church, 'church planting' as a term is relatively new, coming into regular use in England over the last 40 years. The *Breaking New Ground: Church planting in the Church of England* report, published in 1994, was the first formal document in which the Church of England owned 'planting' as a missionary strategy.[53] Where this report saw church planting as 'a supplementary strategy that enhances the essential thrust of the parish principle,'[54] the *Mission-shaped Church* report, published 10 years later, said that this is no longer adequate. 'No one strategy will be adequate to fulfil the Anglican incarnational principle in Britain today.'[55]

Every local church has a 'finite history' whether it was created recently or much longer ago[56] and so church planting is one of the ways the Church of England shares in the apostolic mission of the wider Church.[57] It is evangelism that results in new churches.[58] Former Archbishop of Canterbury, George Carey, said that for the Church of England, church planting has the potential to be an exciting and positive resource for the church.[59]

Church planting is the discipline of 'creating new communities of Christian faith as part of the mission of God to express God's kingdom in every geographic and cultural context.'[60] Contextualisation is 'a necessary and conscious practice of all churches in mission within their own cultures'[61] to enable faithful Christian discipleship in a new cultural context rather than imposing a culture on that context. This is an issue for all churches – in the West as well as other parts of the world.[62] With society in England changing so quickly, many Christians experience mission at home as cross-cultural.[63] The church in the West has a special challenge because this is the first time it has had to mount a mission to a culture that was previously Christian.[64] How do you evangelise cultures that have already received the gospel only to revise or to reject it?[65] Contextual church planting is part of that answer.

A strategic approach to mission must include multiplication. The multiplication of disciples aligns with the multiplication of churches, using similar principles where multiplication is built into the DNA of a church.[66] The thinking behind planting a 'church-planting church' yields an ongoing movement of churches, rather than just planting a single church on its own.[67] Churches that take on this multiplication mindset produce many more churches as a result.[68] We can all too easily focus on new churches needing to become Eucharistic in order to be a 'proper' church. But perhaps the church is not fully church unless it is multiplying.[69]

Revitalisation is the act of planting new life into a dying or dead church. It is a way that a well-resourced church with energetic lay people can help a neighbouring parish that has fallen on hard times.[70] John James, who revitalised Crossway Church Birmingham, lists six reasons for valuing church revitalisations: growing a fresh love for Jesus; building on the past; establishing intergenerational church from day one; empowering forgotten believers; valuing marginalised communities; and uncovering a hidden gospel frontier.[71]

The church in Antioch was invested in by the church in Jerusalem when they sent Barnabas to them (Acts 11:22f). Barnabas found Saul and together they strengthened the church to make it a church-planting church (Acts 13:1–3). In a similar way, resource churches 'are given additional, focused resources with the explicit aim that these resources are multiplied and shared with others. It is expected that, in every sense, resourcing churches will "give away" far more than they "receive."'[72]

It is expected that, in every sense, resourcing churches will "give away" far more than they "receive"

Actively develops a pipeline of leaders for further planting

Resource churches need a flow of leaders who are being prepared to plant and revitalise churches.

An essential element of resource churches is the development of leaders for future church planting and for the mission of the wider Church. Whenever churches are planted in the New Testament, leadership development follows.[73]

The development of leaders flows from the disciple-making of Jesus. Jesus called disciples to follow him (Matt. 4:18–22; 9:9–13; 10:1–4) and invested over three years of life and training in the twelve apostles, giving them authority to proclaim the kingdom of God and to heal the sick and cast out demons (Matt. 10:1f). He commissioned them to go and make disciples, teaching them to obey everything he had taught them (Matt. 28:19) and promising that his presence would be with them always (Matt. 28:20).

Paul was always in the company of ministry colleagues who he trained and then deployed as leaders in various contexts. His leadership development methodology involved a multigenerational programme where leaders were not just taught how to lead in particular situations but also how to develop and train other leaders who could take on that mantle and pass it on to others in turn.[74] Even while Paul was under house arrest and lockdown in Rome, he still mentored and sent out leaders around the world: Epaphroditus, Timothy, Luke, Mark, Demas, Aristarchus, Jesus called Justus, Epaphras, Tychicus and Onesimus are all mentioned in epistles written from there.[75] This is a potent mixture of leadership development, with disciple-making and multiplication interwoven.

Resource churches incubate and train future church planters. Paul describes his role in the growth of the Corinthian church as the planter, 'I planted the seed,' whereas Apollos, as a teacher and encourager, was the one who 'watered it' (1 Cor. 3:6). There is a need to clarify and confirm the call of the church planter.[76] They are often characterised by being self-motivated, catalytic in relationships, entrepreneurial, visionary and able to cast vision that others want to follow, a developer of people, resilient and flexible, and supported by their spouse (if they have one). They need to have a strong emotional intelligence with the character, stamina and adaptability to succeed as a church planter.[77] Church planters need to be those who can shape their church for community, discipleship and mission[78] and enable everyone to get involved using their spiritual gifts so that everyone is on mission. To lead like this in a healthy way means paying attention to their own and their family's self-care. Coaching missional leaders is one of a number of support mechanisms that will help them to perform to their highest potential.[79]

Provides other resources for mission across their city or town

Generosity is one of the core values of a resource church, self-giving for the benefit of the wider church.

Resource churches resource other churches in their city or region with generosity, not to keep resources for themselves but to encourage and bless the wider church. This generosity flows from the character and nature of God himself and taught by Jesus – 'Freely you have received; freely give' (Matt. 10:8), and 'Give, and it will be given to you . . . For with the measure you use, it will be measured to you' (Luke 6:38). Paul encourages generosity in the churches, particularly around financial giving, sowing generously to reap generously (2 Cor. 9:6) and stirring up churches to offer gifts to the poor in the church in Jerusalem (Rom. 15:25–29). Churches are called to give generously to other churches, particularly those in need, not just financially but by doing good, being rich in good deeds, and being generous and willing to share (1 Tim. 6:18).

We see this broad generosity worked out by sending leaders. The church in Jerusalem sent one of its best leaders, Barnabas, to help the church in Antioch, and sent Peter to the new believers in Samaria. The Antiochian church sent Barnabas and Saul to plant churches again and again.

This generosity all culminates for a resource church when it plants churches, giving leaders, congregation members, ministries and funding, and ongoing support and additional oversight, if required, to enable another church to thrive. Additionally, ministries can be multiplied, and resources like books and courses can be made available not just for itself but to other churches too. In these ways it embraces a spirit of generosity so that the wider church is encouraged, equipped and enabled to do its mission more effectively.

Going deeper

These biblical and theological foundations really only scratch the surface, and if you are interested in going deeper, please check out my longer work online at the Gregory Centre website.[80] Resource churches are becoming part of the strategy for dioceses in an increasingly significant way. They are being recognised as playing an important part in the strategies of other denominations and networks too. I finish this brief overview by reminding myself that just as resource churches can be *part of* the church's mission strategy, so the Church of England is a *part of* the one, holy, catholic and apostolic church. There are so many other parts of the beautiful church that belongs to Jesus. Where this fits historically is in the next chapter.

ST PETER'S BRIGHTON

Diocese of Chichester

*At the invitation of the Diocese of Chichester, **Archie and Sam Coates** planted a team at St Peter's Brighton in 2009 from Holy Trinity Brompton (HTB), London. In 2013, St Peter's planted into the Whitehawk estate in East Brighton, and it has now developed into a family of churches in Brighton and Hove with a vision to help people from all walks of life experience belonging and fulfilment as they discover a purpose to love and serve their city. St Peter's has also planted three other churches across South East England. Archie says:*

Before planting St Peter's Brighton, the focus at HTB had mainly been on working with other churches in London and church planting in the Diocese of London. However, in 2007, we heard that the church commissioners were considering closing St Peter's in Brighton due to the diminishing congregation and the building repairs needed. One of our staff member's mothers wrote to Nicky Gumbel and asked him to help in Brighton, describing the huge outcry in the city when the news of the closure broke. St Peter's was seen as the unofficial cathedral of Brighton and over 6,000 people had signed a petition asking the Church of England to save the church. In 2008, Nicky Gumbel met with the Bishop of Chichester and the church commissioners to discuss how HTB could help, and in 2009, we planted a team at St Peter's, with about 50 adults from HTB relocating to the city.

As a church plant ourselves, planting is part of St Peter's DNA, but we weren't looking for opportunities straight away. However, we told our bishop that we'd be happy to help if anything came up, and four years later, church wardens from a local estate church in East Brighton approached us as their vicar was retiring. After conversations with our bishop, we were able to send a team to support the existing congregation at St Cuthman's in Whitehawk and services started in 2013. We are now building a community in the heart of Whitehawk with Sunday services and ministries in the community – including debt counselling, our food bank, youth and kids activities. Our aim is to make the church familiar and accessible to all and help people feel confident to walk into a Sunday service.

When you think about church planting in a city, it becomes clear that one size doesn't fit all. Most cities are made up of small communities and villages, with distinct identities. Not everyone feels at home in a city-centre resource church – some people want to go to their local church at the end of their street. The exciting thing about resource churches is that we can create a family of churches that have similar values and vision, yet reach different people and needs. We have planted twice within Brighton, and these local community churches have distinct communities and outreaches. St Matthias Fiveways in north Brighton has an amazing ministry to young dads called Dadventure, and an event called School Disco for kids, while St Cuthman's on the Whitehawk estate runs food banks, Christians Against Poverty, and a kids club. With our bishop's help, we now have a family of three churches which look different, yet carry the same DNA to share God's love with everyone in this city.

One of the greatest joys is seeing lives being transformed by Jesus. We're putting social transformation and care for the poor at the heart of our churches, and people's lives are being turned around in very practical ways, such as coming off drugs or finding homes. Kerry came through the doors of St Peter's one Thursday afternoon at Safehaven Women, a weekly drop in that we run for vulnerable women in the city. At that time, she was a recovering alcoholic single mother with three small children and struggling to get her life back together again after years of abuse and chaos. Kerry found a sense of home and hope through Safehaven Women, which eventually gave her the confidence to do Alpha and even to begin to come to a Sunday service. She became a Christian on Alpha and was baptised, and has subsequently brought along her parents who have also come to faith. Kerry is now a member of the staff team, working in the area of Safehaven Women with some of her old friends and acquaintances who are still on the streets or vulnerably housed. Similarly, another member of our staff team, Elisha, used to be homeless and now runs the winter night shelter project at Safehaven. We're discovering that the gospel works – people want to come to church to experience Jesus and find a sense of community. I often think of church planting as creating mission stations. Our overall focus is to bless our city and transform society, not simply to create new churches.

Planting is the best form of growing spiritually as well as numerically. Being part of a church plant grows our spiritual life, our giving, our leadership, our participation, as well as growing the Church – it's amazing to look back at the handful of people who came from HTB in 2009 and see their journey. Sending a church plant also grows us spiritually. When we send out teams, it creates space, and the people who stay have to step up and grow as leaders. It reflects the biblical principle of sowing and reaping.

Leadership training has grown organically at St Peter's. We've created a pipeline through building relationships with different members of the congregation and developing lay leaders or students. We run an internship scheme, which can lead people to join our staff team. Some of these leaders might become ordinands and curates, or head up operations and worship for our church plants. A lot of training happens on the job, as we share our DNA and culture and grow leaders through relationships. One of our previous interns at St Peter's, Ryan Fowey, was part of the team who planted Harbour Church Portsmouth and he's now leading a team to plant a city-centre resource church in the capital city of Cardiff. Creating leaders is part of the legacy of resource churches and they can have a significant impact in this area.

The Bishop of Chichester has encouraged church planting throughout the diocese, so it's great to explore opportunities together and operate as one of the missionary arms of the diocese. We work with Bishop Martin, the Diocese of Chichester, and senior staff to plan strategically where we could send a team to plant a church. For example, we planted into Bognor Regis in 2020, which was an opportunity we discussed together as a diocese.

As well as planting twice within Brighton, we have also planted three other churches across South East England. Holy Trinity Hastings launched in November 2014 in the heart of the town, with a vision to be a church for the young, the non-religious, and the marginalised. In 2016, we planted into Portsmouth, at the request of the diocese and Bishop of Portsmouth after they saw what was happening in Brighton, and we launched Harbour Church with a team of 20. It now has a congregation of 700 people across three locations, with services for students and families, and ministries across the city to reach those on the margins. It is also sent a team of 40 to church plant in Cardiff in Autumn 2020. St John's Crawley then launched in 2017 and now has two informal Sunday services, and lots of support for the local community, including counselling, prayer, and services for those on probation.

Local clergy can worry that a church plant will mean that people will leave their congregation. We've found that the main growth comes from de-churched and unchurched people, such as those who did Alpha and never found a church, or those who perhaps stopped coming to church, or people who've recently become Christians through Alpha. Transfer growth does happen but it's often driven by families wanting specific children's or youth work.

In a city like Brighton, there can be two types of church planting: we want to plant in the towns in the diocese, and also create a family of churches in the city. There are around 290,000 people in the city of Brighton and Hove, and typically cities need around 10 per cent of the population to be part of a church to create a tipping point for social transformation. However, our resource church currently couldn't support 10 per cent of Brighton and Hove's population (30,000 people), so we are creating a family of churches in the city, with St Peter's as the mother church, and we're also working in partnership with other churches and denominations across the city. In this way, resource churches can have a significant impact on the social transformation of cities and leave a legacy for future generations.

The Rt Revd Dr Martin Warner, Bishop of Chichester

Archie Coates, in his outstanding leadership of St Peter's Brighton, has been fearless in living out a call to share its resources of people, skills, and funding with other congregations. He speaks of putting out 'empty pots for the Holy Spirit to fill, so that from those newly filled pots others can be replenished.' He is attentive to nurturing a pipeline of ministers who can take this work forward.

St Peter's is a natural landmark in the centre of Brighton. It was built to command, but claims that now it seeks to serve. However, the narrative of service does not always elicit a welcome response.

There are those in the wider deanery of Brighton, and beyond, who see St Peter's as simply an HTB Trojan horse. They question its cultivation of success, its emphasis on youth and students, and its capacity to pull strings with the hierarchy at the very highest levels. They believe that its instincts, if not its stated policies, are homophobic.

But from the perspective of a bishop, I wish to assert that St Peter's is more ecclesial in its thinking than people realise. By that I mean that the priests and people of St Peter's work with the bishop and understand the polity of the Church of England, even if their style of worship disguises that quite well. And Archie has always been insistent that they are Brighton first and foremost.

In the Diocese of Chichester, we encourage the forging of 'apostolic partnerships.' This is, at its best, the embracing by one Christian congregation of the needs of another in ways that safeguard and respect a partner's identity, though that identity might be very different, struggling, afraid, and consequently a bit hostile.

St Peter's Brighton has committed itself to being a blessing to those who live, literally, on its doorstep: the homeless, the addict, the single parent, the LGBTIQ+ person, and especially those suffering from violence. It has sought to become incarnate in the life of an area of acute deprivation and to stay with that commitment, irrespective of the demands and anguish it can cause. Sharing in the life of the poor and marginalised has been a point of growth in the experience of this otherwise successful, articulate, and powerful church.

At present we are working on a Strategic Development Funding (SDF) bid that will contribute resources to St Peter's Brighton and All Saints Hove to be a resource to the wider diocese. Importantly, these churches stand in different theological traditions that are well represented and complementary. We are encouraged by how the task of working together on the bid has already helped them to discover how we all might learn from each other.

Fr Ryan Green, the incumbent of All Saints Hove, represents a thoughtful and constructive critique of the St Peter's model of mission. But the partnership into which All Saints has entered, in the bid for SDF funding, has challenged many of its assumptions. The Archdeacon of Brighton and Lewes, Martin Lloyd Williams, has been skilful in brokering this relationship. There is much to applaud in that partnership, which challenges the stereotype images of both evangelical and Catholic in the Church of England.

But resource churches in Chichester do not only exist in apostolic partnerships with resource churches like St Peter's Brighton. The Catholic wing of the diocese has also been exploring this model, on a local level and with fewer numbers and financial backing and support from the hierarchy of the Church of England.

We have four examples, in Worthing, Lancing, Brighton, and Eastbourne, where Catholic parishes that serve areas of deprivation have come together in an apostolic partnership in order to revitalise a congregation that had grown weary and despondent. When we look back at the history, we see the interesting example of a wealthy parish that founded a daughter church 100 years ago, now being revitalised by the priest and congregation of that daughter church.

We have also benefitted from an initiative that has enabled the Company of Mission Priests, an Anglo-Catholic mission initiative inspired by the work of St Vincent de Paul, to establish a house in central Brighton. These priests offer the opportunity to share and cut costs, pool resources, sustain the integrity of priestly life for a single person, and thereby engage in evangelistic mission in an area of complexity and need.

We have generally been reluctant to designate any church too narrowly as a resource church. We would prefer to ask every church what they can contribute to the enrichment of our diocesan household of faith as a whole. And, of course, some churches are considerably better placed to make that contribution than others.

Concern for the theological diversity of the life of this household of faith is also absolutely valid, as is our urgent attention to the needs of the marginalised and the oblique. Across the ages there are gospel activists who have enabled the poor and marginalised to see themselves as the recipients of God's love, and God's own agents in presenting the mystery of redemption.

It is the responsibility of every bishop to sustain a vision that includes the poor, the vulnerable, the unsuccessful, and the repentant sinner. We have to continue to reach out to the communities of our land, especially to the marginalised communities that feel they are always the recipient and never a resource. 'Theirs is the kingdom of heaven,' says the Lord.

CHAPTER 4

THE HISTORICAL FOUNDATIONS OF RESOURCE CHURCHES

Resource churches are not a new thing in the life of the church in England. The elements of working closely with bishops, working strategically across a city or diocese, planting new churches to reach new people, developing leaders for mission, and resourcing the wider church, all focused in particular churches, runs through all the major periods of the Church through the centuries. I want to explore five broad sweeps of this history and highlight some of these churches and their activities with this in mind. By tracing this behaviour in the past, church leaders and influencers can build fresh confidence and learning for the present.

Early beginnings in Anglo-Saxon England

When Pope Gregory sent Augustine with a small group of monks from Rome on a mission to England in 597, he had high hopes for the conversion of the English. In spite of initial fears, Augustine met with considerable local success, seeing Æthelbert, King of Kent, and most of his court converted and baptised. By Christmas 597, he is said to have baptised over 10,000 converts.[81] From his base in Canterbury, Augustine built Christ Church, established the monastery of St Peter and St Paul, and planted a number of churches around Kent. Was this the first English resource church? From there, missionaries and mission bishops evangelised London, Northumbria and East Anglia with varying levels of success.

Meanwhile, the Christian King of Northumbria, Oswald, sent to Iona for a bishop to evangelise his people. Aidan arrived in Lindisfarne, near Oswald's castle in Bamburgh, and established a monastery. From here, he began to evangelise the North of England, preaching, baptising and ordaining, often accompanied by the king. As the missionaries went out and people came to faith in Christ, they built rough wooden churches for worship. More monasteries were established, like the one at

He began to evangelise the North of England, preaching, baptising and ordaining, often accompanied by the king

Whitby, led by Hilda from 657 to 680. Lindisfarne, and the other monastic communities, became resource bases from which missionaries and church planters were sent to establish the Church in new places.[82] In 653, Penda, King of Mercia, welcomed Cedd and three other monks, allied to Lindisfarne, and they evangelised and planted churches throughout that kingdom. Cedd moved on to Essex where he again planted churches and established monasteries along Celtic lines.[83]

The Roman Church was more organised, with hierarchical structures and demarcated geographic areas, which helped to focus their pastoral work and evangelism, using a unified liturgy with a regular rule of life.[84] Celtic churches grew more organically from an evangelistic mission with people gathering and structures and organisation following afterwards.[85] The Synod of Whitby, hosted by Abbess Hilda at her monastery in 663 with bishops and senior church leaders from around England, brought order to the emerging models with the Church in England turning towards the Roman Church and its structures.[86] Monasteries led by abbots in both movements were evangelistic mission hubs from which bishops led teams of evangelists to witness to new peoples and places.[87] They were centres of learning and a focus of monastic missionary resources, where the evangelistic teams returned from their missions. Around this time, a new kind of semi-monastic, 'minster' church began to emerge, led by a bishop, close to a local ruler and urban centre, with an emphasis of planting churches in the surrounding area.[88]

Dioceses were vast, overseen by a single bishop, and for convenience they were sub-divided in the eighth century into smaller territories led by a minster church in the more important population centres.[89] These minsters, sometimes called *monasteria*, might have been small monasteries served by monks living according to a rule, but increasingly were staffed by secular clerks living in community.[90] The main minster church was most likely the cathedral, where the bishop had his seat, and the many smaller minsters were led by two or three priests assisted by minor clerks, all involved in both pastoral and evangelistic ministry. From these minsters, the evangelistic missions continued spreading out from these centres, and new churches would be formed. With greater missional penetration, local needs became more pastoral and clergy were needed not just on the road but also to minister to new Christian communities as they became established.

The pattern of church growth in the early Anglo-Saxon period was therefore the establishment of a monastic base, led by an abbot with a Benedictine rule, from which teams of monks, under the direction of a bishop, would evangelise the surrounding areas. As people came to faith, small local Christian communities emerged, sometimes building a simple wooden structure to meet in, or gathering around a stone cross in the town centre or countryside. As these grew in number, they in turn would become monastic communities themselves, building a minster church, and become a new operating base for missions further into the kingdom. These monastic minster churches, with a focused number of clergy and lay ministers, also became centres of learning, with manuscript reading and writing, and consequently attracting funds to teach those willing to pay for education. While there was a hot centre of worship, prayer and learning, the energy was focused outwards evangelistically so that more and more could hear and respond to the gospel.

Parish churches began to emerge sporadically as local lords built their own chapels and appointed a resident priest who swore obedience to the bishop, but they had not penetrated villages at this stage. It was not until the latter half of the 12th century that the parochial system was fully established and codified in England and largely across Europe between 900 and 1200. As more and more people came to faith, the number of privately built churches and chapels increased so that by 900, church buildings were widespread and owned mostly by a manor lord, a bishop, a monastery or sometimes the king himself. In 1014, King Æthelred enabled a body of canon law to address the issues arising from the now common parish church. This included four categories of church: the cathedral; the minster; the village church with a burial ground; and the field church (or chapel).[91]

The Church in the Middle Ages

The major shift with the Norman Conquest was in local authority. King William I was a reformer and regarded himself from the beginning as the head of the Church of England, appointing bishops and abbots and calling synods.[92] He appointed Lanfranc as Archbishop of Canterbury and together they strengthened the Church of England and made it more efficient, moving bishops' sees from smaller places to principal towns in each diocese (e.g., Crediton to Exeter in 1050), separating civil from ecclesiastical courts, and standardising the constitutions for all the Benedictine monasteries. Independence from Rome was clawed back by Anselm who succeeded Lanfranc but became an ongoing struggle between church and state, Archbishop and King, for over a century, until the murder of Archbishop Becket at Canterbury Cathedral in 1216, which firmly established church over state. Throughout this time, structural reform deepened and strengthened the Church with higher expectations on the character, behaviour and professionalism of clergy, as well as investing in church buildings as centres of worship and community life.

The early 13th century saw new religious movements, the Friars, sweeping through Europe and impacting England too, most prominently the Dominican and Franciscan orders. The Dominicans as preachers and the Franciscans as ministers to the poor quickly made roots, along with Carmelites and Augustinians, so that by 1300, 169 new religious houses had been established.[93] They brought a whole new energy into the Church as the gospel was preached afresh. However, corruption over charging for services challenged their place alongside parishes and their practices were restricted through the requirement of a licence in 1300.

Rapid urban expansion led to churchgoing habits and discipleship being disrupted or lost so there was a need to re-evangelise a whole generation.[94] I love the intent of Bishop Robert Grosseteste, Bishop of Lincoln, a keen supporter of the Franciscans, who encouraged his archdeacons to grow his diocese numerically and spiritually while he was away in 1244. He told them to preach for conversion, whether people attended church or not, because not everyone was a Christian. In 1246, he then embarked on a two-year visitation of the diocese where he made sure that his clergy were doing the best they could for their parishes. He gathered them together in deaneries and preached to them while other members of his team preached to the people. Everything in Grosseteste's eyes needed to be subordinated to the supreme task of gaining the salvation of human souls.[95]

He told them to preach for conversion, whether people attended church or not, because not everyone was a Christian

The 14th century saw parish churches restored and attended by most parishioners with a revival of preaching that had come with the friars. The church building was by far the most conspicuous building in any village.[96] England was considered Christian and church attendance was high, and in some places, compulsory. But there does seem to have been huge variation 'from the extravagant, intense and devout on one end, to the distracted, apathetic dismissive or hostile on the other.'[97] A large number of chapelries, chapels of ease and chantries were built and funded by groups of lay people because of local demographic changes or because distances were too great at times of difficulty.[98] This caused challenges to some local clergy who jealously guarded the legal requirement for parishioners to attend their parish church.

The post-Reformation church

Church attendance in Tudor times was compulsory with the 1552 Second Act of Uniformity, and the emphasis in this period was more about spiritual renewal of the masses than any development of new churches. The motivation for any church expansion during Archbishop Thomas Cranmer's time in office was to move 'human affections heavenward' through 'scriptural rumination and cultural contextualisation.'[99] One of the important developments was with the publication of the *Book of Homilies*, a collection of sermons used to transmit the new reformed theology to everyday people in their parish churches. And perhaps the most powerful drawing power in evangelism, for Cranmer, was the gospel of free forgiveness itself.

At the beginning of Elizabeth I's reign, many benefices stood vacant because of the brutal turmoil of changing church authority, but they began to be filled again as the country settled into a new rhythm of Christian faith. But a century later, new challenges against the church were led by Thomas Cromwell and puritans with strong Presbyterian leanings against the Stuart King Charles I and the established Church of England. Civil War began in 1642 and King Charles was executed in 1649. Clergy who did not support the puritan cause were ousted from their churches and 2,000 to 3,000 out of the 10,000 clergy lost their livings.[100] The episcopacy was abolished and many clergy had become Presbyterian. But without the episcopacy, there was no organisation or control, leaving the government to issue an order in 1650 to command everyone to attend a place of worship which few heeded. This was followed by another order in 1653 giving freedom to choose where and how to worship. During this period, a growing number of independent sects, opposed to organised religion, grew. Baptists had already broken away. Now Congregationalists grew stronger. The 17th century saw a growth in mysticism and spiritualism and a growing dislike of Presbyterianism such that sects sprang up on all sides. With the restoration of the monarchy in 1660, so too the Church of England was re-established along with the episcopacy. Many new churches were built but sadly this was because of fragmentation.

At the beginning of the 18th century, the church was not dead but had 'slumbered' after the turmoils of the previous two centuries.[101] There was widespread complacency and worldliness of the bishops and senior clergy who were more concerned about personal advancement than pastoral or evangelistic ministry, so the Church was left without any real leadership when it desperately needed it. A small group began to gather to protest against the state of the Church and society, including John and Charles Wesley and George Whitefield. John Wesley had experienced a spiritual awakening that culminated in his 'heart strangely warmed' at a prayer meeting in Aldersgate, London in 1738.[102] From that moment, he, along with other so-called Methodists, began to preach enthusiastically about the need for salvation and a personal encounter with the living God. Converts were organised into

The Church was left without any real leadership when it desperately needed it

discipleship systems of classes and bands, and lay leaders were developed to form an apostolic movement that sought to empower and release every person in the church. During his lifetime, he travelled more than 250,000 miles, preached over 40,000 sermons, and led thousands of people to Christ. By the late 18th century, there were 100,000 members with more than 10,000 class and band leaders, with almost an equal number of other leaders.[103] It was the most disciplined, cohesive and self-conscious large body of people in England. But by the time Wesley died in 1791, the Methodist church was already starting to fragment into different 'connexions.' When they left the Church of England, their lay leaders were simply ordained as clergy in their new denominational sects. What might have happened if this extraordinary multiplying discipling movement had taken root in the Church of England?

Victorian models

In the Church of England, two examples of waves of church building highlighted different responses to shifting demographics. Charles James Blomfield, Bishop of London, sought to address the need for many more churches to be built to meet the expansion of suburban London. In 1836, he created a fund for 'the building and endowment of additional churches in the metropolis' with the goal of building 50 churches at once.[104] Support was not universal for this approach. Thomas Chalmers had led a church extension movement in Scotland which built more than 220 new churches between 1834 and 1841. He said, 'The bishop's scheme is on too grand a scale . . . let him show the effect of the parochial system in one great parish and he may then proceed by degrees to other parishes . . . otherwise his whole scheme will be nothing more than a devout imagination, impossible to be released.'[105] However, by the time he retired in 1856, Blomfield had built 200 churches in the diocese. He explained his reasoning for creating new churches:

> I build churches as a means to an end. I considered that to build a new church in a district where the means of public worship were wanting was a sure way of increasing the number of clergymen in the district that would be a centre from which would radiate all around the light of the Gospel truth and the warmth of Christian charity in the various benevolent institutes etc.[106]

Nationally, Professor K. D. M. Snell's 19th-century social history of England describes the huge numbers of new ecclesiastical parishes being created. Between 1835 and 1896, almost 7,500 new ecclesiastical parishes were formed, including 193 parishes in 1844, and 113 parishes in 1866. One fifth of all

Anglican churches were built after 1801. Between 1835 and 1875, new churches were being completed at a rate of one every four days. The number of Church of England churches and chapels increased from under 12,000 in 1831 to well over 17,000 in 1901.[107] It was truly a boom in church planting.

Between 1835 and 1875, new churches were being completed at a rate of one every four days

One local response was the creation of the 'Islington Church Extension Society' in the evangelical parish of St Mary Islington, London. Church accommodation at the time could not meet demand. On 18 March 1827, for example, with four Sunday services, they had to turn away 400 people.[108] They had already built three new churches to meet population expansion, but it had now risen from 42,000 to at least 140,000. The new society proposed the building of 10 new churches within six years with a capacity of 1,000 seats each, recognising that even this would only meet a quarter of the population's needs.[109] Five to 10 churches were built every decade until 1895[110] making a total of 38 churches planted from the original parish church. As a church positioned for resourcing others, it also created the College of the Church Missionary Society, which was the Church of England's first missionary seminary in 1825.

Just a few years later in 1839, a new Anglo-Catholic church building project focused on the poorer areas of Bethnal Green with support from the Tractarians.[111] Enabled by Blomfield, they raised funds to pay for 10 new churches to be built in the parish of St Matthew's Bethnal Green. By 1854, £115,000 had been raised, 10 new churches built, clergy provision had quintupled, and the annual total of baptisms had increased from 768 to 2,030.[112] There were considerable challenges locally with controversial appointments and financial issues such that it came 'close to disaster', but its legacy was profound. Indeed, it shows that church planting was, and still is, in the DNA of the Anglo-Catholic tradition.

Models in the 20th-century

The period between the two world wars is often regarded as a time of decline in the Church of England, following the aftermath of the First World War. While there was a slow start, the Diocese of London began to act quickly to address the issue of the fast-growing Middlesex suburbs. The Forty-Five Churches Fund was created in 1930 to support the planting of new churches for new people in this part of London.[113] Churches were quickly built but their visibility did not dominate the urban landscape as they were built on side streets. In spite of this, 90 per cent of these churches became viable in their own right, as their clergy worked hard to attract new families.

The building of new Church of England churches continued after the Second World War when population changes meant that some parishes had significant numbers and needed to be subdivided. If a second church was built, perhaps to reach a new area of housing, or an existing church building remained in the parish, they were called daughter churches and new team ministries were formed to enable each church to be led by an ordained minister.[114] Dr Joseph Elders from the Cathedral and Church Buildings Division of the Church of England says that less than 10 per cent of its 16,000 churches was built in the 20th century.[115] If many were built pre-Second World War, then this amounts to approximately 800 churches nationally. Even though this represents the most recent activity of Anglican new church buildings, it is a pale reflection of Victorian ambitions.

A number of Anglican churches began to be more intentional about church planting towards the end of this period and into the 21st century. Here are just five churches from different parts of the country, engaged in different contexts.

- **Holy Trinity Brompton** has planted some 35 direct church plants and many granddaughter and great-granddaughter plants since 1985. One feature of HTB, and some of its larger plants, is of nearby parishes being connected together legally to form one parish, with multiple sites.[116] This 'multi-site' approach enables the base of the church to grow enabling local revitalisation and greater growth, impact and ability to send more teams to plant other churches.[117]

- **St Mark's Haydock**, a 'blended mixed economy church,' planted both fresh expressions of church and a church plant in Wigan. It worked with the Liverpool Diocese to develop a strategy called 'lakes and rivers,' combining the mature ministries of a parish church (the lake) with 14 different fresh expressions of church (the river) in a local primary school, old people's homes and other parts of the community.

- **St Helen's Bishopsgate**, in the City of London, has planted 20 churches since 2001, some 'within the auspices of the Church of England, some outside of it.' It has focused on multiplying lunchtime workplace ministry churches like St Nicholas Cole Abbey, planted in 2006. Other St Helen's plants use the 'Grace Church' umbrella, planting in locations where lunchtime members gather locally to where they live. Some of these churches have been planted independently and then, after appropriate conversations and with willingness on all sides, they are given licences to operate as Anglican churches using a Bishop's Mission Order.

- **St Michael le Belfrey** in York has recently been appointed as a resource church by the York diocese, but it has been involved in church planting since the 1980s, with more recent church plants like G2 and revitalisations at St Barnabas Leeman Road and the Groves in York, and most recently planting a resource church in St Thomas' Newcastle.

- **St Paul's Shadwell** was planted in 2005 from HTB and went on to revitalise four churches in Tower Hamlets by 2014, and supported church plants in the Dioceses of Southwark and Chelmsford, as well as in Paris and Vienna. In 2004, before the planting activity, there were 72 people attending these churches on a good day. By 2015, there were 735, a 10-fold increase in 10 years[118]. Two of those churches have gone on to plant again in Tower Hamlets and in Newham, in the neighbouring diocese of Chelmsford. This church planting is enabling church growth not just in London but around the country and overseas.

Historically rooted

When something new comes onto the scene, some people are naturally suspicious, asking the question, 'How do we know if this is going to work?' It is a good question to ask, and we can never be completely sure of the answer in the short term, but if we can cite historical precedence, it goes some way to strengthening the case for it. For resource churches, we can cite the early Anglo-Saxon city-centre cathedral churches, the Celtic mission centres, the medieval minster churches, the monastic mission movements, the multiplying disciple-making movement of Methodism, the Victorian church extension societies, and the daughter-church movement of the post-war period. They make a strong case for this model working in England again, and help us to reflect in a deeper way about how we might further develop resource churches today.

ST GEORGE-IN-THE-EAST

Diocese of London

St George-in-the-East is a resource church in the Diocese of London. It is an Anglo-Catholic parish, harnessing the potential of community organising to grow inner-city churches, rooted in their neighbourhoods. More people now attend each week – all within walking distance of the church – than at any time since the Second World War. **Fr Angus Ritchie and Fr Richard Springer** *write:*

Late in 2014, the Centre for Theology and Community (CTC) moved into the East Crypt of St George-in-the-East. Simultaneously, the Bishop of Stepney at the time, the Rt Revd Adrian Newman, was reviewing whether the church had a long-term future, as the weekly congregation had dwindled to under 20.

CTC was founded to harness the potential of community organising, when rooted in prayer, to renew congregational life and help churches act with their neighbours for social justice. To move into St George's at this point presented both a challenge and an opportunity: could these methods be used to renew a congregation at such a low ebb?

There were lots of reasons to think it would be difficult: the neighbourhood is 60 per cent Muslim; and the parish is right next to a thriving Holy Trinity Brompton plant (which was led by Bishop Ric from 2005 to 2015!).

Our journey of growth began using the usual resources – a stipend and a house – very differently for an 18-month experimental period. We used the stipend to pay for two part-time clergy (Fr Angus Ritchie and Fr Tim Clapton) from May 2015 and then housed a lay community in the rectory from September of that year.

The growth began almost immediately, as we reconfigured the way we worshipped. The 20 of us no longer rattled around a large building but gathered around the High Altar. If you were new it felt intimate and joyful – rather than a sad echo of past glories. New people began coming straight away, before we had even started anything. We did one-to-ones with everyone who came to find out why they were coming. Local people came, who were not Christians but who were seeking community in Shadwell. When they came to faith, there was a new energy and sense of belonging.

Community organising has been important to us, with its principles of starting with one-to-ones, putting people before programmes, and helping people discern and draw out their own passions and vocations. The social action campaigns we have been involved in, like the affordable housing campaign, have also grown our congregation. One baptism family said that they had not been looking for a church, but when they heard that this church was leading an affordable housing campaign, they had decided to come along.

We're growing, not by being predatory, but by being porous – the practices of community organising help us to build relationships in the neighbourhood to challenge injustice, and also to be a more welcoming church and develop those who come as leaders and disciples.

The Catholic practices of daily Mass, of Adoration, of the Examen all make us take time to be still before God. Even though we might be seen as an activist church, there is actually always plenty of room to wait, to pull together the strands of what is happening. It is not just that they are good ideas, but they are grounded and embedded in prayer.

After 18 months, we decided together that the experiment was working – that the parish should once again have a rector (which is why Fr Richard was recruited to the team in 2016), with lay workers living in other flats.

Community organising, rooted in prayer, was helping us to grow the Sunday congregation and to act with our neighbours for justice. The next step was to plant new worshipping communities to reach those who don't make it through our doors on a Sunday.

If 70 per cent at the local school were Muslim, then what about the families of the 30 per cent? How could we take church to them? That is how Choir Church started – with music lessons each Wednesday, teaching religious music, which was sung at a monthly midweek Mass. We now have 30 to 40 people at that monthly service – and several families have come to faith, and now come to Sunday Mass as well.

We have also started The Open Table (building community organising for justice, and worshipping with and for homeless people) and Nossa Voz (a Portuguese-speaking congregation of hidden and low-paid workers). Like Choir Church, these are both worshipping communities in their own right and are teaching us how to make Sunday Mass more fully inclusive of the people who live and work in our parish.

It was a real step of faith for the PCC when St George's became a resource church in 2018. Over time, this grew, and the church began to think of itself as being able to offer gifts to others. There was a shift in people's minds: there was an increase in the numbers coming, but we were not simply aiming to win a 'numbers race' but were, rather, aiming to play our part in God's renewal of the wider Church.

We want to help churches aiming for people within walking distance, to help them flourish, to grow from 20 to 70 people. We are asking ourselves, "Where else can reinvigoration happen?" Community organising is helping us to discern vocations in different kinds of Christian leadership among people the Church often overlooks. We're excited about the part they will play in this renewal.

The Rt Revd Dr Joanne Grenfell, Bishop of Stepney

I was delighted to know, when I began in post as Bishop of Stepney in July 2019, that Stepney Area already had a resource church: St George-in-the-East, in the modern Catholic tradition. I was already used to working with resource churches and church plants in my previous role in Portsmouth Diocese. I had seen the way that they could be a catalyst for growth in depth, impact, and numbers. I had worked happily with churches in an evangelical tradition, and had particularly encouraged them to be deeply rooted in their communities, to serve those in need in areas of challenge and deprivation, and to listen to local colleagues of different church traditions, so that they could operate with open doors and open hearts for all local people.

It felt right that my predecessor, Bishop Adrian Newman, had designated St George's as a resource church. The 19th-century Anglo-Catholic revival was grounded in London's East End. The 21st-century revival that we need to see today has to be able to address again issues of poverty and deprivation, and also to challenge us to see the ways that people are marginalised now because of, among other things, ethnicity, class, immigration status, gender, and sexuality. We need to speak into these issues, while offering beautiful, participative liturgy, which allows us to glimpse the majesty of God, who is at the heart of human flourishing, the source of all justice and of peace. St George's does that work today in the East End. It is highly diverse and inclusive, not just in token ways. People are seen as individuals, their gifts and their confidence nourished. Food is served – oh my, the fried chicken and dough balls! – and people are enfolded in love through hospitality, whether on the streets at a Monday Open Table or gathered in church after a large Sunday service. Everyone is sent home with extras lovingly wrapped in foil trays.

St George's is a greenhouse for community organising, developing community campaigns and growing community leaders. It has seen growth in numbers of disciples by drawing people in through community organising, and it has also seen growth in depth of discipleship, by sending Christians out to serve and agitate for change in the world. The numerical growth may not be as fast as we see in some other resource churches, but it is substantial and it feels deep and lasting. I now see St George's encouraging other small, modern Catholic churches to grow in similar ways: by being rooted in the local, by building capacity among local people, and by living out an incarnational faith. There is something for us to learn from this model about creating capacity in local leaders, and doing this work with individuals patiently and respectfully, seeing their agency and encouraging them to discern together how and where God is calling them next.

I have long believed that resource churches are at the heart of the wider growth of the church. I am glad that we can see different – complementary, not competing – models of that growth.

CHAPTER 5

THE IMPORTANCE OF RESOURCE CHURCHES

Resource churches are playing an increasingly important role in the Church of England – a new kind of church in a landscape that is wary of change. They are not the only kind of church we need, nor are they better than other churches, but I believe they have a vital role to play.

The missional context in 21st-century England

Why do we need resource churches? Where do they fit into the missional landscape today? For me, this always begins with recognising the enormous missionary challenge in front of the Church in England. At the time of writing, Anglican attendance represents 1.5 per cent of the population. Overall church attendance nationally is approximately 8 per cent. According to the Faith Survey, church attendance was 10.3 per cent of the population in 2013 and is forecast to decline to 4.3 per cent by 2025, unless trends change.[119] The greatest challenges lie in the largest urban areas where Anglican attendance drops to 1.2 per cent per capita.[120] This drops even further in inner-city estates. Urban areas, where 83 per cent of the national population live,[121] have far fewer clergy per capita.[122] Cities have been underinvested in by the Church of England for many decades, resulting in less ministry and consequently lower attendance. Investing in city and town centres is therefore a strategic decision for dioceses and for the Church of England. This does not mean that rural areas are less important, rather that, in relative terms, urban areas have been neglected.

To address this challenge, mission and growth in the church can be achieved through revitalising struggling churches, developing the growth of existing churches and planting new churches. This, of course, includes the need for a renewed focus on evangelism, discipleship and social transformation, underpinned by worship, sacraments and prayer.

The case for growing the church

In my travels, I often come across the complaint that we should not focus on growth, especially in terms of numbers. I think this is because we are trying to make sense of the overall decline of the Church in England over the last century and because it takes the focus away from the small, beautiful acts of God that can so easily be missed if we only value numbers.[123] Growth is not one-dimensional. We must value growth in depth of relationship with God and with one another, and we must value growth in terms of the impact the Church can have on the world, especially in local communities. But we must not shy away from valuing numerical church growth.

We must not shy away from valuing numerical church growth

The parables of the kingdom, taught by Jesus, point towards the growth of the kingdom when the gospel is preached. The mustard seed is the smallest of all seeds, yet it grows an enormous tree towering over a garden (Matt. 13:31–32). When a sower scatters seed on good soil, it multiplies 30, 60, or even 100 times what was sown (Matt. 13:8). When the gospel is preached there should be an expectation of growth in terms of people responding to the gospel.

This growth should be measured in many dimensions – in depth of commitment and discipleship, in being faithful and being present, in making a loving impact on the community, and in number, with more people responding to the gospel. Beth Green and Tim Thorlby helpfully describe the national Church growth debate in general terms that include these three measures.[124] They are important for every church, including resource churches. There are many examples of 'spiritual measures' combining all of these attributes together, including personal spiritual growth, and are better covered elsewhere.[125]

However, sometimes there is no growth. In fact, a 2019 research study conducted by Lifeway Research for Exponential[126] suggested that 35 per cent of churches in the United States are declining, with a further 35 per cent plateauing in numbers (see figure 5). Figures in England are likely to show more decline.

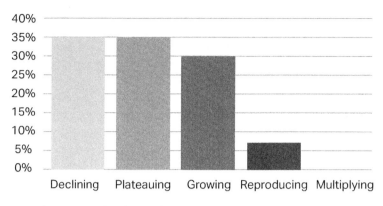

Figure 5. Change in US church attendance since 2016.

Surely death and decline are not supposed to be normal for the church? We need a recovery of the apostolic DNA of the early church so that the gospel can be communicated afresh in our generation and the church can grow again. I am constantly amazed that church growth principles are not taught in our theological colleges and are rarely reflected on seriously in dioceses and churches. Every church tradition has stories of growth in their histories that should be celebrated but also re-evaluated in the light of today's very different contexts. I value and want to commend the various church growth initiatives and courses that are supporting churches and dioceses willing to recognise that they need help to change and develop their thinking and practices to see growth in all its dimensions. If you haven't already, do check out the Grow Course at the Gregory Centre for more details.[127] This is not just for keen churches. Surely every church should be concerned about growing itself.

The case for church planting

Wouldn't it be fantastic, imagining – and praying – for a moment, if the church in England doubled in size, from 8 per cent to 16 per cent of the population? That would be a tipping point in terms of influencing and impacting the whole nation. That would be revival. But what about the remaining 84 per cent of the population? Jesus commanded his disciples to go and make disciples of all nations (Matt. 28:19). With this command in mind, we still have most of our nation to reach! Church growth is important, but it is not enough. We need to plant new churches in new places to reach new people in new ways.

We need to plant new churches in new places to reach new people in new ways

Church planting is about starting a new church in a new place, 'planted' from elsewhere. It picks up Paul's language in 1 Corinthians 3:6, 'I planted the seed, Apollos watered it, but God has been making it grow.' 'Church Planting' as a term is a relatively new one in the church – perhaps used more in the last 50 years and not much in church literature over the centuries. But it is something that has been going on for centuries. It is the very essence of how the Church has grown around the world. Every church was planted when it first began.

Church planting is important because

1. it reaches more people, going beyond the existing reach of the church;

2. it reaches new people, who would not normally attend churches that are ministering already;

3. it releases new leaders with new energy at the chance of being involved in addition to the existing leaders ministering in existing churches;

4. it increases the growth potential of the church because there are more places reaching out to more people than was happening with fewer churches;

5. it is more able to design everything around new people and those exploring the faith.[128]

Revitalising existing parish churches, by sending a leader and a team of people, has a similar impact, bringing new missional energy and reproductive potential. Therefore, church planting can play its part in addressing the problem of church decline.

There are many types of church plants and all are needed. Different types of churches reach different types of people. Small, local churches are able to be very specific in a particular ministry to their geographical area or people group. Larger churches reach different kinds of people who are looking for a larger church experience and who are prepared to travel for that. Some churches are traditional, others are contemporary. Some are sacramental, others more orientated around teaching and preaching. One parish church cannot reach everyone in its parish, though its Anglican incumbent might have the 'cure of all its souls'.[129] If it is attracting 1.5 per cent, and other denominations attracting another 6.5 per cent, there is plenty of room – 92 per cent more room – for other churches too, that might connect in different ways to reach different people.

I believe that every church can be involved in starting or planting new churches, sending leaders and people in a team to reach a different group of people. At a local level, adopting a sending approach to growing the church has the potential to lead to new churches being created. Rick Warren, pastor of

Saddleback Church in California, encourages this approach, saying that healthy churches should measure their sending capacity not their seating capacity.[130] Research by Peter Brierley in 2012 showed that church growth in London had increased significantly since 2005 by 16 per cent, largely attributable to Black churches and other immigrant churches and larger churches growing. The study showed that one church in seven (15 per cent), had started another church within the last 20 years, with 93 per cent still meeting. Pentecostals had started the most, followed by Anglicans. Two-fifths of the growth was reckoned as people not previously church-goers.[131] Planting churches leads to church growth!

Different planting approaches and models

One reaction to my encouragement to all churches to get involved in church planting is that it's only for larger churches. But the evidence says otherwise. Lots of different kinds of churches have been involved in church planting and pioneering, and they have used a whole range of different approaches and models depending on a whole range of factors in the sending church and the context it is planting into. Different missional networks will focus on particular models, but to reach everyone, everywhere, every kind of model will be needed[132]. These include:

- Reopening closed churches
- Revitalisations
- Multiplying congregations
- New development areas
- New churches in schools
- Churches in urban estates
- Workplace gatherings
- Café churches
- Community space meetings
- Missional communities

Earlier items in this list might be more likely to be led by clergy and might include paid staff. Later items might be more likely to be led by lay people and have unpaid leaders. I believe this is going to be shaken up in the next few years with more so-called 'bi-vocational' church leaders, who might have a different profession, perhaps giving them an income, alongside leading a church or church plant. If that's you, or someone you know, keep exploring this avenue for leadership in the church.

Within this list, resource churches are more likely to be involved in reopening closed churches or revitalising struggling churches and almost certainly multiplying congregations to reach new people in different ways. This approach is more likely to lead to larger congregations and churches than some of the smaller focused models. This also means they will cost more as a model (because of staff and building costs) and therefore they need to pay attention to covering their costs as well as putting aside funding for new planting of this kind. This partly explains why they have a higher profile, both in terms of visibility, planting and growth capacity, and income and expenditure costs.

I want to stress here the point that resource churches are not better or worse than other models and approaches in the missional landscape. Fresh Expressions of church have exploded in number and impact across the country since they were first noticed at the beginning of the 2000s and described in the seminal *Mission-shaped Church* published in 2004. There are now more than 2,800 'Messy Churches' in England, founded and overseen by Lucy Moore since 2004, reaching new families in all-age congregations.[133] There are 1,500 Church of England-appointed pioneers creating new ways of doing church in their communities. Researcher Canon Dr George Lings includes 'traditional church planting' in his spectrum of fresh expressions of church and I know plenty of church planters who would include fresh expressions of church in their definition of church planting. The point is this: that there are many forms of church planting, fresh expressions and pioneering, all working in the vast mission field of the unchurched and the Church needs all of them!

Towards a culture of church planting

A mindset of incremental growth alone might be inadequate. The Scriptures point towards multiplication as a way that growth can happen, leading to more prolific results. The first command to human beings in the Scriptures is to 'be fruitful and multiply' (ESV Gen. 1:28). After the flood, Noah is encouraged to 'be fruitful and increase in number; multiply on the earth and increase upon it' (Gen. 9:7). The new Adam, Jesus Christ, builds his church (Matt. 16:18) and the church after Pentecost grew quickly through new disciples coming to faith (Acts 2:41; 4:4; 5:14; 6:7; etc.). The number of churches planted across Asia and Europe grew quickly too as the gospel was proclaimed and churches planted (Acts 19:10; Rom. 15:19b). Multiplication of churches should be normal.[134] Some have gone further to say that if there is no reproduction of churches, then that church is sterile.[135] So while there is no explicit command from Jesus to multiply churches, the natural and emerging instinct of the church, as described in Acts, was to reproduce itself.[136]

The greatest transformation in terms of reach into the mission field comes from creating multiplying churches or church-planting churches.[137] A church that has church planting in its DNA will not just plant churches itself, but plant churches that plant churches in a continuing, multiplying way. This approach requires being intentional about creating that kind of reproducing culture.[138] And when you're intentional, extraordinary things can happen.

A church that has church planting in its DNA will not just plant churches itself, but plant churches that plant churches in a continuing, multiplying way

I love mathematics (I know it's not everyone's cup of tea!) and I love playing around with geometric progressions. That's where you have a progression of numbers with a constant ratio between each number and the one before, like doubling numbers in a series 1, 2, 4, 8, 16, 32, 64, and so on. It shows that if you keep doing something in a particular way, the results begin to multiply fast (see figure 6). If you change the ratio, like planting more often than every three years, the total numbers accelerate even faster. My friend Dave Ferguson leads the Newthing Network in the USA and they became intentional about the multiplication of churches. He told me that each church in the network tries to plant a new church every year. They send a church plant leader and an apprentice leader. The apprentice, like an Anglican curate, learns on the job and then plants a new church, taking a team with them after the one-year 'residency.' Of course, when they plant, they too take an apprentice with them and the sending church takes on another new apprentice. That is intentional!

Year	0	3	6	9	12	15
No. of churches	1	2	4	8	16	32
	•	••	••••	••••••••	•••••••••••••••••	••••••••••••••••••••••••••••••••

Figure 6. Multiplication of churches where each church plants every three years.

Resource churches can behave like this when they are given planting curates who keep planting so that struggling churches can be revitalised, and new areas can be planted into. Other churches might not be able to do this at the kind of scale of a resource church but nevertheless can still be involved in training church planters and sending them out to plant new churches. When this kind of practice catches on, a culture change takes place, where church planting is no longer seen as something odd and unusual but rather completely normal for every church.

So how do we get there? My experience over the past few years has shown that church planting can be developed in a diocese if specific interventions are made to move it on from a passive approach to an intentional, then strategic, approach until it is normative and there is a culture of planting (see Figure 7):

- *Passive approach*: a diocese has a 'permission-giving' culture where occasional opportunities arise, and planting happens almost by chance.

- *Intentional approach*: a diocese sets church planting goals, and it is affirmed as a ministry option for clergy and lay leaders. Existing church-planting energy is leveraged or imported from elsewhere. Some churches are appointed as resource churches and church planting is mentioned in diocesan strategy.

- *Strategic approach*: church planting is part of the growth strategy of a diocese and owned by the senior staff. Significant planning addresses difficult-to-reach places and redirecting resources (people, buildings and money) for a missional end. A foundation of prayer leads to diocesan structures being aligned to support church planting, setting more ambitious goals, identifying planting opportunities proactively, identifying and training church planters and aligning diocesan policy and practice with the church-planting plans.

- *Culture of church planting*: every church is involved in planting fresh expressions, missional communities and planting teams to reach new people in their parishes. Multiplication is the norm.

Passive approach	More intentional approach	Strategic approach	Planting culture
A few plants; not well-supported, sometimes discouraged	Church-planting churches created	Many plants happening (especially in key locations)	Multiplication across the diocese

Figure 7. Developing church planting within a diocese.

At this point, there are a small number of dioceses who are actively using a strategic approach to church planting using these definitions. And there are none, in my opinion, where there is an active culture of church planting. There is still some way to go!

The calling of a resource church

So, a resource church is a church-planting church that has this kind of planting and multiplying mindset in its DNA. Ideally, their bishop appoints planting curates to them where they learn their trade before being sent to plant or revitalise other churches, taking a team and funding with them. When they plant, they take an apprentice planter with them, who learns about planting as they plant, so that in time, they will go on to plant themselves. If a standard curacy lasts three years, then planting curates could be planting and revitalising churches every three years. Reproduction and multiplication are at the heart of their DNA. And these churches are growing, reaching new people in new places with the gospel of Jesus Christ. In this way, resource churches and their plants join in with the diocesan strategy of growth and impact, evangelisation and social transformation.

With multiplication in its DNA, a resource church will naturally have an area-wide, city-wide or town-wide vision. To support this, it will develop a pipeline of leaders for further planting, alongside its own leadership development practices. As a church that is determined to play its part beyond its parish to the wider area, it will use its own ministries and resources for that mission by generously offering them to the wider church.[139] With a church like this, they can be invited to join in with some of the strategic conversations alongside senior staff of dioceses, knowing that resource churches can be part of the solution to some of the challenges they face.

As resource churches are created, I believe it is important to differentiate them from other churches. They are not merely a large church; large churches may not have planted or necessarily have the desire, attitude or vocational capacity to plant in this way. They are not merely a church with lots of students, though many resource churches have been intentionally planted to city centres in order to reach the concentrations of students in those places.[140] Being designated as a resource church is not a badge that is used to honour a church that is favoured over others. And, though many churches might be called 'minster churches,' they do not necessarily behave as the minster churches of former centuries that were missional centres sending teams to evangelise and plant new churches in their regions. Neither is a resource church just a parish church with an important calling or vocation limited to reach and minister to its parish locally, incarnationally and tactically.

By contrast, a resource church's calling is to reach beyond its parish as it plants other churches and resources mission in the wider area. It is therefore strategic, city-wide and extra-parochial.[141] It develops a culture supportive of planting, and prepares to plant, training leaders and teams and saving and setting aside funds. Once planting opportunities are identified, the resource church supports the planting team before, during and after the plant.[142] Parish churches are not required to give away their people and resources in the same way.

The place of prayer and planning

How does all this happen in practice? When you try to do something new in an institution, there is an inevitable resistance to that change summed up by 'institutional inertia.' Nevertheless, change is important and necessary.

That change starts with prayer. It is a spiritual change that needs to be discerned and brought before God. In that place, hearts change, motives align and courage is imparted. Prayer fans into flame something new, something extraordinary, something supernatural. Prayer gives us new perspective and vision and anchors us in the very purposes of God. Prayer changes things.

Prayer fans into flame something new, something extraordinary, something supernatural

In a recent conversation with Bishop Sandy Millar, he told me that he was convinced that nothing would have happened at HTB without prayer. He recounted how Jeremy Jennings as prayer director there set up corporate prayer meetings three times a week with additional meetings alongside those. Everything was prayed into, from encountering God's presence, to the finances, to evangelism, to church planting, to every aspect of the church's life, and of course for the nation and nations. Effective intercession must be diarised so we can hear what the Spirit is saying, just as the Spirit of God told St Paul where to go as he planted churches throughout Asia and Europe.[143]

On that foundation of prayer, we can start to plan, to consider the possibilities, to count the cost. We do need courage to challenge the status quo and it is no surprise that resource churches might do that. That planning needs to be local and strategic, and we encourage every church to do the Church Planting Course so they can be as prepared as possible for all that lies ahead. Strategic planning involves setting goals for planting, identifying opportunities across a diocese, identifying leaders and training them, and aligning diocesan policy and practice so that there is not a continual struggle to enable this to happen easily and proactively. I will cover more on this in the next chapter.

PRESTON MINSTER

Diocese of Blackburn

*At the invitation of the Diocese of Blackburn, **Sam and Hannah Haigh** were sent with a team from Holy Trinity Brompton (HTB), London, to relaunch Preston Minster as a resourcing parish in September 2019. It is part of a new project led by the Bishop of Burnley, Philip North, combining the two existing parishes of Preston Minster and St George's Preston. Its vision is to be a church that offers a big welcome and a safe space to explore and encounter the person of Jesus Christ. Sam says:*

I sometimes get asked, 'What are resource churches and where did the idea come from?' It's a concept that we see in the Bible – St Paul set up churches in strategic cities that reached the villages and towns in the surrounding areas. But resource churches are also part of our Anglican heritage. In the 1800s the priest of Preston Minster (formerly the parish church of St John's) planted five churches around Preston during the industrial boom. We often talk about this legacy during our services. It's exciting to connect the congregation with their church's history, showing that church planting is part of the life and DNA of Preston Minster. Our vision to start new churches in Preston feels like a continuation of this parish's story.

We planted in September 2019 from HTB, London, at the invitation of the Diocese of Blackburn as part of a new project led by the Bishop of Burnley, Philip North. We have become a resourcing parish, bringing together the two parishes of Preston Minster and St George's. St George's is led by Fr David Craven and is rooted in the Anglo-Catholic tradition, whereas Preston Minster's worship style is charismatic evangelical. We're not merging or trying to change each other's styles of worship, but instead we work closely in partnership and learn from each other. We find it helpful to remember that 'good fences make good neighbours.' For example, Fr David at St George's is involved in Catholic renewal movements but is also able to draw from the HTB model of church planting, with the hope of planting or revitalising struggling Anglo-Catholic parishes in the future. Bishop Philip, who is also from an Anglo-Catholic tradition, has been extremely supportive and we meet with him regularly. It's a partnership of friends and it's been really encouraging working together so far.

Our methods of evangelism look different across this new resourcing parish: St George's might hold an outdoors service of Mass or public Ash Wednesday service, whereas our focus at Preston Minster is more on street evangelism or Alpha. But we both share a sense of wanting to be present in the community and this common missional focus holds us together. There's definitely a sense that the congregation at St George's is being mobilised and becoming more outward facing, and it's been really encouraging to see early signs of growth there. We know we'll need different types and traditions of churches and church plants to reach the whole city of Preston. Some people won't connect with Preston Minster and its style of worship, so St George's might be the right place to help them with their journey of faith. We want to release each congregation to be true to its tradition so we can play our unique part in reaching people across the city.

We're already seeing lives being changed since we launched Preston Minster. One lady called Charlotte came to the pre-launch gathering at our house. She had a vague Christian background but neither she nor her husband had settled in a church. After the pre-launch gathering, she attended the launch service and rededicated her life to Christ that day. She is now fully part of the church community, engaging in mission and living out her reawakened faith.

Colin and Amy, a couple in their mid-20s, would walk past Preston Minster whenever they went to The Warehouse, a nightclub next door to the church. They wanted to get married and had always thought that the church was a beautiful building on the outside, but they'd never seen inside this church or any church before. One Sunday, they decided to come along and they were blown away by the welcome, the message, and the whole experience. They've been back every week since, they have done Alpha, and are now serving on team. Having found a sense of home at Preston Minster, Colin and Amy love sharing this new faith and hope with their friends. They're brilliant at inviting people to Alpha: they know that it won't be awkward or pressurising so they're confident to bring friends along and share what God's done in their lives.

Our latest Alpha course had 60 guests, and over half of these were people that we've never met before. They'd heard about us from adverts on the buses, flyers, or friends. We're passionate about the re-evangelism of Preston, so we keep this as a high priority in terms of our budget and focus. We've recently launched an evening service to help us connect with more people, especially students, so we've begun by planting internally. It helps us to remember that starting new things is part of our DNA. We also encourage connect groups to look at how they can grow and plant, so that we are creating a culture where it is normal to multiply. Even though we're not sure yet what opportunities will appear, we want to prepare people so that planting is embedded in who we are.

Preston is a historic place, dating back to Roman times, and sits right in the centre of Lancashire. It was only designated a city in 2002, so there's been a lot of development recently in the city, and Preston has worked hard to reinvent itself. There are about 140,000 people living in the city and about

400,000 including the surrounding urban areas. The University of Central Lancashire is a strong presence in the community and there's a thriving student population of over 30,000 here, increasing employment and entrepreneurship. We're excited about working with students as university is often a key time in someone's journey to faith. However, there are still huge needs – Preston has one of the highest suicide rates in the country and there are many issues with homelessness, addiction, alcohol abuse, and deprivation. Our church sits on the cusp of this split – the redeveloping town centre full of energy is on our left, but the clubs, pubs with late licences, and red light district sit on our right. We're sensitively exploring how we can get involved in some of these areas. We didn't want to roll in with our social action projects, so we're spending time listening to the needs of the people around us and to God. Interestingly, Preston was at the heart of the Temperance Movement in the 1800s and the city has an epic Christian heritage. Its name is derived from Old English, meaning 'the dwelling of priests.' There are many Catholic churches and a strong Catholic influence in the Anglican churches too. We're excited about building on this legacy and seeing what God does over the coming years in this wonderful city.

The Rt Revd Philip North, Bishop of Burnley

Struggling town or city-centre churches can be a big headache for a diocese. The size and visibility of the buildings mean that they are often perceived as a measure of the vitality of the Church more generally, so their weakness gives an impression of a Church in retreat and decline.

There are two churches in Preston city centre, the minster and St George's, which have been run as a single benefice for many years. They had benefited from a loving and generous ministry from their former priest, but insufficient resources, both in terms of people and funding, had left both churches struggling for viability. Lying in the centre of the largest city in the diocese, set amidst the shops, nightlife, and civic buildings, and close to the fast-expanding University of Central Lancashire and Cardinal Newman Sixth Form College, this was crying out to be a resourcing parish.

But the nature of this benefice meant we could form a resourcing parish with a difference. The Church of England is afflicted with tedious, tribal dichotomies: Catholic or evangelical; liturgical or informal; biblical or sacramental. In much of the Anglican communion, these dichotomies make little sense. In the UK they can be all-defining and can drain energy away from the mission into circuitous and sclerotic internal arguments.

The existence of two church buildings in the Preston resourcing parish has given us a place where we can tackle such dichotomies and a place where traditions can learn from each other. The minster offers informal charismatic worship with a focus on preaching. St George's proudly retains a strong Catholic identity and is Eucharistic. But both remain in the same parish and are committed to growing together, learning from each other, and drawing on the richness of each other's traditions. This vision has been warmly embraced by Sam Haigh, the vicar, and by the associate vicar, Fr David Craven, who, in the strength of their personal relationship, model the shared ministry we want to see. Our hope is that Preston will be a resourcing parish that can plant or renew churches in both traditions across the Blackburn Diocese.

Absolute transparency, lots of conversations and meetings with stakeholders, and a clear vision meant that Preston resourcing parish was able to launch without some of the opposition that has been experienced in other parts of the country, and the leadership is developing extremely positive links with the city leaders and influencers and with other churches. The Covid-19 pandemic came at a very difficult time, just as the minster was starting to grow to the size and energy necessary to enable planting. But the team demonstrated the most extraordinary agility in the height of lockdown and was able to start a food bank and a meals service which has made a huge impact on local perceptions.

As we look to the future, the project faces a number of questions and challenges. Firstly, while the minster has grown to over 100 regular worshippers, we are yet to learn what sort of strategic and evangelistic flexibility will be required to adapt the resource church model to the context of a working class, Lancashire city which does not have the younger and more cosmopolitan graduate populations upon which other resource churches draw. Secondly, finance and buildings will present formidable challenges, especially given recently discovered cladding issues at St George's and the need for extra space at the minster. It would be a pity to see huge amounts of staff time drawn into the complexities of two concurrent building projects. The tapering out of diocesan and Strategic Development Funding grant monies will also be hard to manage as the presence of a large team is critical if the churches are to continue to reach outwards into communities desperate for physical and spiritual nourishment.

But there are also enormous opportunities. A planting strategy is being developed which will reach across Lancashire and especially into areas where church life is weak. A strong focus on young people in Preston and in the churches that the resourcing parish plants will help us as a diocese to develop ministry into and alongside schools, especially our many Church of England schools. The formation of a new theological college in the North West will give the parish the opportunity to contribute even more richly to the formation of new leaders, and it is our hope that the resourcing parish will be a key player in that development. The sheer energy and imagination that the team brings is role modelling the confident, outward-looking, and entrepreneurial ministry that we would love to see across the diocese.

It would be wrong to see any strategy as the golden bullet. The resource church model is complex and extremely resource-intense and hence expensive, and there will be questions, especially post-Covid, about the viability of direct replication in other parts of Lancashire. But to be able to reinvigorate two struggling city-centre churches with a team intent on communicating in every aspect of its life the joy of the gospel, focused strongly on evangelism and sacrificial in its service of the poor, can only be good news. If people's perceptions of the Church of England are now informed by the energy of Preston Minster and St George's, then hearts will surely be changed and imaginations captured with the wonder of Jesus.

CHAPTER 6

CREATING A RESOURCE CHURCH

The 100 resource churches created by bishops in dioceses around the country by 2020 are now in different stages of growth. Some are thriving, in terms of growth and sending out church planters and teams, while others are struggling to get going or getting stuck in various ways. When a resource church thrives, it can have a high impact on its diocese, turning churches around and increasing the faith and optimism of what is possible. If it is struggling, a resource church can be a drain on time, energy, people and money, increasing confusion and even division. How are resource churches created and how can they be enabled to be as effective as possible?[144]

Creating a resource church involves a number of stakeholders, each playing their part, and a number of key steps that need to be taken. Diocesan bishops are the main stakeholders, who can lead with confidence or reluctance, leading to a successful or stunted process. They need to take the lead in the creation and working of a resource church because of the sheer energy involved in changing the status quo. Diocesan office holders must also get behind the effort to support the resource church leader and their team. If any are reluctant in any way, plans will stutter. Everyone needs to play their part.

There are two ways resource churches are created. For most, it will involve turning an existing larger church into a resource church. Where there is no larger church in a city or town with the capacity to revitalise or plant, it will involve planting a new church, either using an existing church building, fit for purpose in an existing parish, or by finding a non-ecclesial building and converting it for church use.

Where a resource church is being planted from scratch, four stages are involved in the process (see figure 8), along with plenty of communication and prayer throughout each stage.

Figure 8. Stages involved in planting a resource church

Stage 1 – Diocesan commitment

The first stage is for the diocesan senior leadership to fully support the presence and ministry of a resource church.

a. Being clear about why

Once they express interest in having a resource church, the senior team must be clear about the reasons why it is necessary, as above. Essentially, that will be a missional and ecclesial response to their current situation:

- Missionally because there is a need to focus new energy on urban centres where there are fewer Christians.

- Ecclesially because the diocese might recognise the need for a different kind of church than those that exist already.

The investment up front in clarifying and articulating this will pay dividends later on so that there is as broad a consensus as possible about what is needed.

The need for a resource church raises broader questions about investing elsewhere in the diocese as there is a reasonable cry, 'What about us?' This calls for a wider strategy to be developed that goes beyond a previous generation's approach. It used to be enough to make sure each church was thriving, through good leadership, healthy practices and good relationships in their deaneries. But with so much decline across the national Church, a different approach is called for, where simply managing that decline is not an acceptable strategy. The needs of today call for a strategy of investment in mission and growth. This inevitably means choosing where to invest and where to divest. Of course, this is challenging for those at the sharp end of divestment, but it is necessary so that those same places receive missional investment in the future. Focusing on resource churches is part of that strategy, where future planting means that previously under-resourced places can be revitalised.

A wider strategy will include a range of investment and planting options:

- Resource churches revitalising parishes again and again.

- Medium-sized churches revitalising one or more parishes.

- Churches of all kinds exploring planting opportunities on estates and in unreached parts of their parishes led by lay leaders.

- Churches fostering fresh expressions of church in their parishes.

- Small scale multiplication of churches led by lay people.

When set alongside a range of options, a resource church strategy makes sense.

b. Identifying a potential resource church

Alongside engaging the diocesan senior team, the bishop must identify a potential resource church. Ideally, a resource church will be revitalising and planting churches again and again over many years, as an engine of renewal in the diocese and beyond. That requires a certain size of church that has the capacity to repeatedly send out leaders and teams and funding. Perhaps more importantly, it requires a leader and PCC who are excited about this kind of generosity, who can lead the church through the considerable change challenges involved, who are great trainers of planting curates and teams, and who have a good working relationship with their bishop. The church also needs to be in a location where an influx of new members can fuel future resourcing over time, and this is most likely to be in a city or large town.

If this kind of church and church leader are already present in one of the cities or towns of the diocese, then the bishop can explore with them whether they are called to this kind of ministry. This will involve turning a larger church into a resource church (see later in this chapter). If there is no obvious church for this potential role, then a new church might need to be planted and built up by an incoming resource church leader – stages 2 and 3 below.

c. Communicating the vision and purpose clearly

It is crucial for the bishop to own the decision to create a resource church because they have the authority to make it happen in practice. They must therefore ensure that it is fully part of the vision and strategy of the diocese. There is too much at stake for this to be a pet project on the side when it relies so much on diocesan structures and local church leaders for it to succeed. This will require a bishop to build momentum carefully through the right channels, setting the tone for this strategic approach, with colleagues getting behind it too.

The decision should be communicated to all those involved, including the diocesan senior team and other diocesan officers, and when appropriate, to any directly involved in the deanery, starting with the area dean. There are a number of objections that may need to be addressed and these are explored in Chapter 9.

Bishop David Urquhart was clear that Gas Street Church had a clear part to play in the Birmingham Diocese vision where it was one of four strategic strands. Bishop Sarah Mullally announced the creation of 19 resource churches in London Diocese after a clear process where every church in the diocese was given an opportunity to apply to become one. The invitation also included the opportunity to explore being revitalised by one of these churches, to which a number of churches responded. Communicating the wider strategy is key.

d. Allocating planting curates

The core purpose of a resource church is to revitalise parishes by planting churches. When a resource church is involved, it sends a planting curate with a team and funding to revitalise the struggling parish. Therefore, in order to enable this, planting curates should be allocated to the resource church. This is essential, even if there is resistance in the diocese. If this does not happen, it makes it difficult for the resource church to develop the momentum necessary to build the vision and strategy needed to sustain planting again and again. The easiest way to do this is to allocate a proportion of the existing diocesan allocation of training curates to a resource church so that it can train them in preparation for planting.

Alternative funding might be possible, either from Strategic Development Funding (SDF) or from the resource church themselves, allocating some of their budget towards this. In the early years of a resource church's life, this is very challenging on their own funding, and is risky because the diocese does not have any obligation to place that curate into a planting situation.

Mature resource churches might be given several planting curates if they have the capacity to keep planting with them. The benefit to a diocese is that those curates gain experience in the context of a larger church where there is extensive practice and experience of church planting. It is interesting to note that most of the planting curates from Holy Trinity Brompton (HTB) who have planted resource churches have led their churches into significant growth perhaps because they have learned the skills and developed an expectation of leading into churches of this size.

Stage 2 – Pre-planting planning

To create a new resource church, there are a number of tasks that the bishop, and the resource church leader, need to do to ensure everything is in place for a successful plant. The key components to plan are:

a. Identifying the leader

The key task in creating a new resource church is finding the right leader. Bishop Paul Williams has remarked to me that leading a resource church is one of the most challenging leadership tasks in the church today. These leaders are under huge expectations to plant something from scratch, lead through several stages of growth, develop leaders to 'give away,' and do it again and again. There are not many who have the leadership competence, character, capacity and calling necessary. Planting a resource church requires a high level of all these attributes, and in practice these leaders are usually found in churches that already understand the dynamics involved, that is, in existing resource churches that have a track record of planting churches and developing leaders. (See Chapter 7 for more on this.)

Once a new resource church leader is identified, it is helpful to have an interview process, so that all parties are clear about what they are taking on. The timings of this appointment might be blurred because so much depends on where the new resource church should be located and when it should be planted. The main factors directing the timing are the alignment of a good leader who is ready, the identification of an ideal location, and the diocesan team being on board.

Once appointed, they should be given a point person in the senior team to link with, a clear set of goals and expectations, and enough freedom to get on with making decisions about what is necessary for a successful launch.

b. Finding an appropriate building

The diocese needs to identify the right building for the resource church. It could be an existing church building, with a clear mandate for change, or a neutral space that can be consecrated for worship. Factors to be considered are:

- Location – close to places with a high footfall and good transport links.
- Multiple rooms – the church will need small group rooms for children and youth work, as well as offices and ministry spaces.
- Flexible space – fixed furniture like pews inhibit the space from being used 24/7 for ministry, and other rooms enable different uses throughout the week.
- In good order – sometimes buildings need development to get them fit for purpose. The more that is done up front, the less the church will be distracted by building development, and the more it can focus on being outward facing for growth and impact.

Birmingham Diocese could not find an appropriate church building for a resource church it was keen to create so it bought an old gas works warehouse, with brick and wrought ironwork fittings. It was refitted for ministry, funded by a combination of SDF, a diocesan loan and congregational funding. Within five years, Gas Street Church had a membership of close to 800 and has planted a number of churches with more in the pipeline. St Thomas' Newcastle was planted in 2019 with just 20 members into a church building located on the intersection between two universities and a college. With a new focus on ministry to students and young people, it has grown rapidly and in 2021 began plans to revitalise a church on a nearby housing estate.

c. Agreeing the legal structures

Legal structures must be carefully addressed in advance of any problems that might arise. Three scenarios are worth considering:

- *When using an existing parish building, with the leader appointed as the priest-in-charge:* there are no additional legal requirements for the new resource church. If there is an old PCC, the oversight relationships will need to be negotiated between the old and new groups, since new members cannot join the PCC until they have worshipped at the church for at least six months, in order to qualify for the electoral roll, and then be elected before the April church annual meeting (APCM). There are workarounds, such as being able to co-opt up to one third new members on to the PCC. This is critical for releasing funds, making decisions about Sunday services and ensuring good communication and relationships between old and new.

- *When using a non-church building in the parish, with the leader as the priest-in-charge:* creating a separate legal entity might be helpful in order to separate the new ministry from the existing parish ministry. In such a case, a Bishop's Mission Order (BMO) can be used which enables a separate charity (a Charitable Incorporated Organisation, or CIO) to be formed to enable a separate bank account to be created. The BMO can have separate trustees from the parish, though having some crossover might be helpful for continuity.

- *When using a church or non-church building within an existing parish but not to be a part of that parish:* a BMO is required to separate the ministry and governance so that the new resource church can get on with its mandate to grow and plant from there. A CIO would be created to enable a bank account to be opened. Additionally, a set of protocols would need to be drawn up to help manage the relationship between parish and resource church that would include using parish registers, leafletting and communications, and regular meetings.

d. Developing the funding plan

There are considerable upfront costs associated with creating a resource church, including finding the right building, making sure it is fit for purpose, then funding the cost of ministry, including allocating planting curates. In any assessment of costs, it is important to consider the return on investment.

When a parish church is revitalised, the church begins to grow again. That can happen with a good leadership appointment, but when it is combined with a team being sent with a mandate for change by the bishop, that growth is accelerated significantly. When the planting team comes with a sacrificial giving mindset, this impacts the overall stewardship of the church, and financial giving and voluntary serving increases. When staff appointments are made, especially when they are configured towards growing the church community, this accelerates growth even more. As the church grows, the costs are covered more quickly, as growing numbers of people start giving. If some of these staff roles are paid in advance, this enables church growth and church giving to increase more quickly than if they were appointed later.

As the church grows, the costs are covered more quickly, as growing numbers of people start giving

If building development costs are to be borne by the resource church themselves, they are likely to be burdened by this for years and this will likely distract from their chief task of growth and planting. The revitalisation of parish churches made by resource churches will save costs in the long term and so it is worth exploring alternative funding for these initial building costs. It is essential to cost the project fully, without taking short cuts, so that the detailed necessary costs are known in advance. A number of dioceses and resource churches have stalled because of unresolved costs of tens of thousands of pounds not being planned or accounted for.

Ministry costs should be borne by the resource church itself. However, when a resource church is planted, it takes time for these costs to pay for themselves, as outlined, so upfront funding helps a church like this to start up and accelerate its growth. In time, with good teaching on stewardship and financial giving, the church pays not just its own costs but begins to put funding aside for future church planting. With both building development and ministry costs, a simple calculation shows that if a heavily supported parish is revitalised by a resource church paying its own ministry costs, it can easily save a diocese £0.5M over 10 years.[145] If there are multiple plants from a resource church, the cost savings quickly mount up. Set alongside this, the increased impact on the mission and ministry in this parish, and the investment, seems very reasonable. Therefore, dioceses should plan to fund these, alongside the resource church leader, and apply for Strategic Development Funding to accelerate what is possible.

If there are multiple plants from a resource church, the cost savings quickly mount up

In this second stage, the new resource church leader will be recruiting a planting team, both from their own sending church but also from a wider pool, and preparing them for planting. Staff are recruited and detailed planning is done to work through the first 100 days, which are usually quite pressurised and unpredictable, a two-year plan to ensure that the key building blocks are put in place, without needing to deliver everything upfront from the beginning, and a five-year plan that will include the first plant from the resource church. This planning is all covered in the Gregory Centre Plant Course.[146]

Stage 3 – Launch and grow church

This simple heading belies the challenges of doing this in practice! From my own experience of church planting, I know the amount of love, sweat and tears involved. At the Gregory Centre, we have spent years developing practical tools and training to help leaders and teams navigate this vital stage.

Careful attention needs to be paid to launching well, with good communication and energy. The resource church will focus on evangelism and discipleship, strengthening the congregation, developing leaders, structures and staff, and praying for God to open doors for the gospel, change hearts and pour out his Holy Spirit. A simple but practical action is to start praying, preaching and preparing from the start to be a church-planting church, including having a budget line for planting in the accounts from day one.

The bishop should ensure that the resource church leader is well supported, including coaching and mentoring, and that good communication is in place between them. The bishop should also ensure that the diocese continues to develop its church-planting strategy and within that to identify future planting opportunities.

Stage 4 – Planting from the resource church

This stage is covered in the next chapter in more detail. In brief, the diocese brokers the relationships with the receiving church and sorts out any particular legal structures. It provides seed funding for the plant and addresses building issues. The resource church sends the planting curate with leaders, teams and seed funding and supports them before, during and after the plant. Over time, the resource church develops a pipeline of leaders to do this again and again. And the diocese aligns its policy and practice to support a church-planting strategy.

Turning large churches into resource churches

So far, we have looked at the stages involved in starting a resource church from scratch. However, in perhaps the majority of cases, the strategy will involve turning an existing larger church into a resource church.

A large church is not a resource church. They differ in what they focus on. Large churches tend to attract and nurture disciples from beyond their parish boundaries. But the way a diocese treats them affects their ability to resource others and this, in turn, affects the way they see themselves. For a large church, the missional aim will be to grow and disciple its congregation, whereas the aim of a resource church is to evangelise a city. A large church has excellent preaching, quality production, intentional discipleship and high-impact social transformation. A resource church will aim for these things but will be more focused on developing a pipeline of leaders who are ready and willing to be sent out. Larger churches are often good at encouraging stewardship and so are seen as a source of income to be distributed by the diocese. Conversely, resource churches can be seen as a diocesan resource to revitalise other churches and plant new ones. Large churches have limited planting activity on an opportunistic basis, if the diocese allows it. Resource churches have a proactive strategy to plant churches.

The aim of a resource church is to evangelise a city

I have met a number of church leaders who would like to consider being a resource church but there is a reticence on both the bishop and their own sides because of their history together. Previous bishops may have restricted the activity of larger city-centre churches because they might have stepped beyond a strictly parish ministry. At the same time, bishops might have treated these larger, well-resourced churches as 'cash cows' for the diocesan Common Fund.[147] These church leaders may have come to resent these limitations and felt restricted in their ambitions for the kingdom of God. Therefore, there may be some leaders and churches that are obvious choices for being a resource church but there may be a few historical challenges and perspectives to work through and this may need time and brokering by a third party. For many places, it is much simpler, and church and church leader are ready to respond positively to an invitation by their bishop to fulfil such a role.

The potential resource church leader and their PCC and leadership team need to be clear about what is involved for them. They must have a vision for working with the bishop and the diocese to see renewal and revitalisation of churches beyond their own church; they must count the cost of such work, giving away leaders and funding to ensure the church plant is as strong as it can possibly be, and they must ensure the whole process is founded and sustained by prayer. This vision requires a practical strategy, with goals for recruiting and training planting curates, recruiting and training lay teams, regular planning meetings with the diocese, and clarity around expectations, timings, funding and communications.

Once appointed, the bishop's team and the resource church leader's team work together to identify the first church plant or revitalisation, and, in time, will move onto stage 4 of planning and planting their first church.

In practice, to turn a large church into a resource church involves two of the four stages above. It needs a diocesan commitment to plant through them, together with the church's own desire to plant, and to go through the sacrificial process of sending the planting leader and team. While there is not the requirement to plant a brand-new resource church, there will still be effort involved in reorientating itself to plant rather than just be a larger church. It will be a significant cultural shift.

Figure 9. Appointing an existing church as a resource church.

Just because two stages are avoided, it does not necessarily make it easier for a larger church to become a resource church. Years of not planting means that the idea of giving away leaders and people and money runs against a culture of trying to grow and keep existing members through more or better programmes. This is a fundamental change in DNA to get this buy-in and culture change, requiring significant effort to see it through over many years (see figure 9).

For success, the leader and the congregation of the large church must share a vision to be a resource church, and everyone must be on the same page.

- The bishop must designate the church as a resource church in order for everyone to understand what is going on.

- The diocese must have a church-planting strategy to identify opportunities for future plants and revitalisations. It must develop a clear strategy to invest in the revitalisation of the city/town by creating a resource church, alongside their other initiatives, and should provide the church with planting curates to prepare for future planting.

- The resource church aligns its culture and practice to the church-planting strategy by preparing congregation members to be sent, allocating a budget line in its accounts, identifying a pipeline of ordained and lay leaders to plant, and supporting the team before, during and after the plant.

- Finally, to realise the planting opportunities, the resource church provides leaders and teams and seed funding for its plants while the diocesan leadership team broker the relationships with the receiving church/parish/deanery, sorts out the legal structures, addresses the building issues and provides seed funding.

Addressing the change issues

Creating resource churches presents major change issues for a bishop, their diocese and for the churches getting involved. By definition, this will be disruptive to a system that is either in decline or is unused to change. Making any changes or treating some churches differently to others must be thought through and prepared for well. But it is essential for change to happen.

The challenges for the resource church are to keep the vision alive and cultivate extravagant generosity, to give away their best. They need wisdom to deal with other parishes' concerns, fears and sometimes even anger. They will need to move from start-up to large church to planting church, all of which requires exceptional leadership skills. And they need to prepare well for recovery after planting so that, in time, they can be ready to do it again.

The challenges for a diocese involve aligning practice with strategy. They will need to be self-aware enough to identify unhelpful, seemingly unchallengeable practices and be creative with them. And they will need to be prepared to deal with parishes that express fear, concern or anger, whether accusations of unfairness or concerns about empire-building. See Chapter 9 for more on this.

Why bother?

With so much to address, is it worth it? Unequivocally, yes! I believe we cannot afford *not* to do this. Resource churches have shown that if created well and followed through with good integration into the diocesan vision, strategy and structures, they can be an enormous positive change agent in a diocese, leading to church growth and revitalisation. And, as you can see, story after story in this book has shown this to be true.

ST GEORGE'S LEEDS

Diocese of Leeds

*St George's Leeds was designated as a resource church by the Bishop of Leeds at the licensing service for **Revd Lizzy Woolf** in 2017, making her the first female leader of a UK resource church. This opened a new chapter in the life of a large, gathered, city-centre church, particularly known for its work with the homeless. Revd Lizzy writes:*

St George's has a worshipping community of around 800 people,[148] including 100 students, 150 children and young people, 50 Farsi speakers including asylum seekers (our morning services are simultaneously translated), young professionals, older adults, plus more than 100 people with multiple and complex needs (including homelessness, addiction and mental health crisis) who are part of our fresh expression known as Lighthouse. We aim to take a city-wide strategic view in all our ministries, partnering with others wherever possible.

St George's is part of a wider resource church programme in Leeds Diocese, which has accessed the Strategic Development Funding. For St George's, this has meant a seat at the table and ambitious targets for both growth and planting, but no money. I meet monthly with the other resource church leaders and our area bishop, working together to bless our city, and greatly value their friendship and encouragement.

Our first church plant was in January 2018 to St Paul's Ireland Wood, a parish around five miles away, with a congregation of around 25, facing closure. We sent our curate to be the new vicar, with a team of 48 people (many of them local to St Paul's), and a gift of £50,000. In their first year, they grew by an additional 30 people, started a toddler group which now connects with 120 families, and built partnerships with local organisations to bless their local community.

Back at St George's, we released the planting team with great rejoicing, but there was also a need to regroup. There was loss to process and gaps to fill; the congregation responded magnificently, stepping up to serve and lead. The most challenging issue has been replacing the regular giving that went with the plant (about 10 per cent of our annual budget). After two years we have made progress but still have quite a way to go. As we tackle this, we are learning about changing attitudes to money among younger generations and are uncovering many discipleship and pastoral issues. Finance is currently our key limiting factor, but we are learning to balance faith with realistic wisdom, and to choose generosity.

Our next major church plant is planned for 2022, and we are working with our area bishop to identify a strategic location. In the meantime, we are developing smaller partnerships using different models. For example, we were recently approached by the vicar of a small, declining church in North Leeds, asking if we could help. We invited him to come to St George's to share his vision for a new contemporary congregation. Four young adults, who live near that church, responded; two were on our worship team, and all four were small group leaders. Two months later, we commissioned and sent them out to join him, doubling the size of his team.

We are currently working on two major mission partnership initiatives with the neighbouring parishes on either side of St George's, one to reach students living in the Hyde Park area of Leeds (which we believe has the densest population of students in the UK), and one to reach those working in the city centre (using a landmark church building which currently stands empty). Both will be hugely stretching and challenging but offer great kingdom opportunities.

We are also investing in training: expanding our intern programme to include other churches across the diocese (in partnership with Leeds Diocese and New Wine), sharing expertise from Lighthouse to enable others to start similar ministries (in partnership with Leeds School of Theology), and offering training and coaching to church planters (in partnership with St Hild Theological College).

We are excited about what God is doing in Leeds and the North of England and are delighted to be able to play a part.

The Rt Revd Paul Slater, Bishop of Kirkstall (Area Bishop for the City of Leeds)

It's early days to be able to speak about the long-term impact of the Resource Church Programme in Leeds, especially as we still contemplate the full effects of the pandemic.

We have five Resource Churches across the city and a number of small plants and substantial plants either completed, or well on the way, in terms of planning and knowing the destination. A key element of our strategy has been to think across the whole city of Leeds and not have our vision constrained at all by Deanery boundaries.

I have been enormously impressed by the commitment, resilience and wisdom of our five Resource Church incumbents and much of the gains have come as a result of their work in very different contexts. We have good working relationships on the Resource Church Board, with some robust conversations and a key person has been our Programme Manager, who has a very strong commitment to the vision.

We are learning all the time. For example, we have identified how we need to plan further ahead so that planting curates can see at an early stage a specific pathway for their development and ministry.

One of the contributions made by the Resource Church Programme is a realisation that a much more intentional approach to growth is needed across the whole city of Leeds. We remain committed to territory as an Anglican principle and to revitalising churches so that they can be real places of Jesus-shaped hope in their communities.

The Rt Revd Nicholas Baines – Bishop of Leeds

Resource churches form part of our strategic approach to church growth and planting in a sustainable way in a diverse diocese. St George's was the obvious choice for starters as we had been talking with them about planting for many years. I do have some misgivings about flogging a single model where context demands a variety of different models (rural, differently urban, suburban, etc.). However, strategic thinking means that questions about context, resourcing and people have to be worked through thoroughly in the planning.

As always, challenges involve finance and people. St George's (our first) is very well led and our expectations are being met. The group of resource church leaders in the diocese is proving to be a very impressive group who meet regularly and frequently. Obviously, resource churches are one model and they may not be adaptable everywhere. But where they do have capacity, they are an essential element of any growth strategy.

CHAPTER 7

PLANTING WITH RESOURCE CHURCHES

Resource churches are designed to revitalise and plant churches. They have responded to an episcopal invitation. They have stepped forward believing it is their vocation to do this, despite the sacrifices. There will be considerable effort involved on the part of the diocese, the resource church and the planting team. But it is worth it because of the impact, growth and missional energy that can be released at every level over time as other churches find their place to join in with the wider strategy of planting and revitalisation.

As we explore planting with resource churches, there are parallel and complementary routes for diocesan senior staff and for resource church leaders and planters. This alone calls for a joined-up approach with plenty of communication as each area is addressed and developed. In my experience, the planning process needs to cover 10 areas, which may seem like overkill, but if they are all addressed systematically, most issues will be anticipated and many future problems will be avoided.

Developing a theological vision

If you are going to embark on anything that involves change, and therefore likely resistance, it is very helpful to know why you're doing it. When the knocks and bruises come your way, you will be able to remind yourself why you started this and why it's worth it. That will hopefully keep you going! In the Church, we need to have a theologically based vision for church planting, and it needs to be widely owned in your church and in the diocese. We covered some of this in Chapter 3.

We need to have a theologically based vision for church planting, and it needs to be widely owned in your church and in the diocese

A resource church needs audacity for a God-sized vision that longs to see him transform lives and communities for the better; generosity as it gives away leaders, teams, resources and funds for planting; humility as it engages with the diocese and local churches, depending on the power of the Holy Spirit; unity with the wider Church, seeing that it is only part of all that God wants to do through the whole Church; and tenacity to keep going, never giving up on all that God has prepared in advance for them to do. These values can be embraced by the resource church as it prays and dreams of all that God wants to do through them.

A diocese must develop an understanding that it is called to continue Jesus' call to go and make disciples, by forming new communities of faith, reaching everyone, everywhere. It can encourage every church to get involved in reaching their parishes to connect with new people in new places and new ways. And it can encourage some churches to use their calling and capacity to plant beyond their parishes to revitalise struggling churches and evangelise new unchurched areas. From this understanding, it can begin to envisage a renewed diocese, looking for new ways to adapt to the ever-changing missional context. It is worth taking the time to set out clearly why resource churches are part of the theological solution to this huge opportunity.

Founding the vision in prayer

We know that prayer changes things and that Jesus calls us to ask, seek and knock so that we can receive, find and have doors opened to us (Luke 11:9–11). We see the early church asking for boldness to preach the word and heal the sick (Acts 4:24f). We see Paul admonishing the churches he has planted to keep praying in the Spirit on all occasions with all kinds of prayers and requests (Eph. 6:18). Pray, pray, pray!

I have found it so encouraging when people pray into church planting. When we planted our first two churches in Tower Hamlets from St Paul's Shadwell, our prayer leader, Kerst, led a team to prayer walk around the two parishes involved. They discerned that we should approach each plant differently, one with a clearly sent team showing great love and generosity, the other approaching it slowly, with great sensitivity and care, admonishing me with the words 'slow burn'. We acted on this and it was exactly what was needed. We believed that God had spoken to us and guided us.

Prayer for planting should be on the agenda of resource churches and diocesan teams every step of the journey and beyond. It might mean giving the responsibility to someone to coordinate it so that specific requests can be made to God. Remember James' words on prayer, 'You do not have because you do not ask God' (James 4:2). Found your vision in prayer.

Setting goals

I believe that if you want to get things done, especially if you have a big vision, you need to set goals. A goal helps to focus what you are trying to do. It helps with planning. It provides motivation and inspiration for everyone involved. And it provides a measure so that it can be evaluated. I use SMART goals most of the time – specific, measurable, achievable, relevant and time-bound – but just having any kind of goal is better than none.

Do you have a clear goal relating to church planting? Resource churches can set goals around how many plants it aims to start over a specific period of time. Goals can be set around the leaders needed, the training required, the funds to support it and stage posts along the way. A diocese might begin with an overall goal of a particular number of plants over a period of time. This can then be broken down into goals about different types of church plants – resource churches, parish plants, church revitalisations, plants onto estates, small church plants, and so on.

In London Diocese in 2013, we set a goal to create or renew 100 new worshipping communities by 2020. This helped us focus on what we needed to do and specifically how we might go about it. By the end of 2020, we had planted 87, hampered only by the Covid-19 pandemic. But given that it had taken 28 years to plant 50 churches before 2013, we saw that goal setting accelerated church planting in London by a factor of seven. London was the first diocese to do this, but others followed, with Leicester Diocese setting a goal of 300 to match the number of parishes, and Oxford Diocese aiming for 700 more Christian communities. Astonishingly, by the end of 2020, most dioceses had set church planting goals that totalled 3,500 new Christian communities of various kinds. Who would have thought that was even possible a few years ago?! In order for a goal to be met and celebrated, it needs first to be set!

Releasing church-planting capacity

Once a church has planted once, there is the inevitable question of whether it can do it again. If it already has a vision for planting, it will be thinking how it can release its full potential to do it again and again without damaging itself long term. One of my favourite sayings of Sandy Millar is, 'Don't kill the goose that lays the golden egg.' In other words, be careful how you plant, so that you can do it again healthily and sustainably. To do this well, it will involve working out a natural rhythm of planting, so that leaders are replenished, the church is enabled to grow back to pre-plant figures, and funds are built back up. I think the most important factor is to have a flow of leaders which I cover below and in the next chapter.

From a diocesan point of view, the question is about scale. Does the diocese have enough churches with the planting capacity and intent to fulfil the scale of ambition it has for growth? I have seen that having a resource church in a diocese is a catalyst for this kind of thinking. When Harbour Church Portsmouth was being explored, I remember having a conversation with Mike Duff, the vicar of nearby St Jude's which had been praying into and exploring the idea of planting themselves. He effectively said, 'What about us? Can we do this too with the diocese's blessing?' The answer was a resounding yes and space was enabled for them to start planning and planting alongside the planting of Harbour Church itself. Within a couple of years, Crofton Parish Church on the other side of the diocese was appointed as another resource church. Between them, eight churches are being revitalised.

A diocese must think about how it can increase its capacity to church plant. This will take time, but it can do this by investing in or creating church-planting churches and working with them over time to prepare them for future planting. It can also encourage every church, of whatever size, to consider small scale plants within their parishes to reach different groups with fresh expressions and pioneering initiatives.

Encourage every church, of whatever size, to consider small scale plants within their parishes to reach different groups

Identifying church-planting opportunities

The next step is to identify church-planting opportunities. This is best done collaboratively between resource church and diocesan senior team. Ideally each team will come up with their own list of possibilities and then compare notes, seeing which might be mutually possible. I prefer a list of possibilities to be explored rather than a single offer as it puts too much weight on one option when there might be several that are better if considered together.

I have encouraged resource church leaders to study a map of their area and prayerfully think through where there might be obvious places to plant. That might be where clusters of existing members already live, where the core of a church-planting team could be more local, or it might be along transport lines that people use to go to and from the resource church, whether by public or private transport. The map we drew in Shadwell went along the train lines going west to east and north to south and we plotted congregational membership along these routes. In the end we planted along bus route lines and main roads, but the mapping got us started.

The bishop is able to explore these opportunities with a bird's eye view of the whole diocese. There are two main areas for him or her to carefully look at – large parishes with not enough churches or struggling churches that could be revitalised. For large parishes, a planting intervention might be required. For example, in Notting Hill, London, where there is a combined population of 30,000, there are six parishes, with average attendance of 100 people in each church. A few miles away, in Feltham, there was one parish church with 100 in attendance, within a population of 30,000 people. Very simply, there was a need for more churches in Feltham, where the likelihood having more churches was likely to lead to higher church attendance. So, the Bishop of Kensington invited St Stephen's Twickenham, a local resource church, to plant a new church in Feltham town centre using a Bishop's Mission Order. That church is now growing with no loss to the other church.

Where churches are struggling, or where the mission potential is not nearly being met, there might be a case for revitalising that parish. The easiest time to do this is when a church goes into vacancy, giving a natural pause to reflect on what is best for the church and where bishop and PCC can work through options that might include a partnership with a resource church. I like the way in which Bishop Martin, the Bishop of Chichester, describes this as an 'apostolic partnership' which holds the dynamism and optimism of an active, missional relationship. [See Appendix 2, the Impact vs Feasibility Matrix Tool, for identifying church planting priorities.]

The first step for a bishop then is to develop a list of places that could be planted into and churches which may be suitable to receive a planting team. This could take place collaboratively with a bishop's senior team where knowledge of parishes and clergy movements might be well known. There are also bottom-up opportunities where deaneries can map their areas, identifying places to plant to as well as clarifying potential parishes where change is needed. In London Diocese, we offered, alongside a number of other options, the chance to be revitalised by a resource church and this was explored by a number of parishes.

If the mapping work has been thorough, dioceses will be ready for the opportunities when they arise

When it comes to identifying the most obvious opportunities, opportunism is often involved because timings cannot always be predicted. However, if the mapping work has been thorough, dioceses will be ready for the opportunities when they arise. Therefore, it is best to be prayerfully strategic. To do this, senior teams can identify the largest parishes or areas with the lowest church-attending populations; the poorer communities, not just the 'easy' places; and the new and unreached communities, not just revitalising existing or closed churches. The balance needs to be struck between what will give the greatest impact and what is easiest to do in practice (again, see Appendix 2). Feasibility questions might include: Is there local support to plant in the area? Is there the infrastructure to plant there? Is there anyone with the resources to plant there? Parishes and locations can be mapped onto an impact vs feasibility matrix to prioritise the choices available. Locations with high impact and high feasibility represent the best choice for planting. Locations with high impact and low to medium feasibility can be noted in case circumstances change and the feasibility increases.

Producing a comprehensive planting plan

So, once you have established the planting capacity and the opportunities that might be possible over time, you will need to make a plan with the most feasible plants that will have the maximum impact. This means agreeing a list of places including the best locations for a plant, and existing churches suitable to receive a plant or graft. When any of these existing churches goes into vacancy, presentation should be suspended immediately to signal that its future is under review.[149] Priorities should be identified in terms of which churches should plant where.

After a church-planting strategy workshop, Paul Slater, Bishop of Kirkstall (covering the city of Leeds), drew a rough map on a flipchart of what he could imagine in terms of planting opportunities and possibilities in the Leeds area. He then drew together a group of resource church leaders and potential church planters into a learning community to make plans and pray together. A few years later, many of those dreams had become a reality.

A communications plan can be developed to ensure that relationships with receiving churches, parishes and deaneries are brokered well

Once the planting plan is in place, a communications plan can be developed to ensure that relationships with receiving churches, parishes and deaneries are brokered well, giving time to work all the issues through. Planning ahead enables the financial, building and legal issues to be faced and addressed.

Establishing a leadership pipeline

Now that the resource church has a plan to plant at a particular rate, and the diocese has an overall plan of where and when it might plant and revitalise churches to strengthen and grow the Church, a deployment plan needs to be worked out. Do you have the number of church planters you need to meet your plans?

To think this through, I have found it is helpful for resource churches to draw up a 10-year timeline and to mark on it when plants ideally might happen. After that, you can work out when you need to recruit the planter, which might be up to three years in advance. And then working out when you need to start looking for that person, which could be four years before the actual plant. That's why it needs some planning (see figure 10) and some early conversations with your bishop!

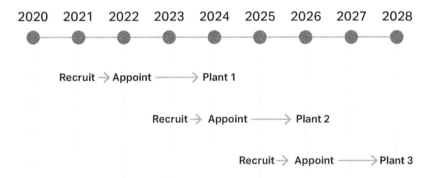

Figure 10. Drawing a planting timeline to determine your leadership pipeline needs.

From a bishop's point of view, the diocese needs to work out its leadership requirements to fulfil the planting aspirations. How many ordained and lay church planters are going to be needed over the coming years? How can resource churches and other planting churches be supported to ready themselves to fulfil their plans? Where will they be recruited from? The best place for church planters to be trained is in church-planting churches, so curates and ordinands need to be deployed to those churches so that they will be ready when called upon to plant. Developing leaders for planting is covered in the next chapter in more detail.

Increasing the capacity to deliver

Once resource churches and dioceses consider planting churches at scale, they need to make sure that they have the capacity to deliver this consistently. Most resource churches appoint an operations manager to think through all aspects of administration and organisation in the church. In addition, more mature resource churches might recruit an associate vicar to assist with the day-to-day running of the church. This frees up both the resource church leader to focus on developing mission and ministry opportunities, and dealing with problems and obstacles as they arise, as well as planting curates who can focus on learning in a growth environment and preparing to plant.

Diocesan senior leaders must be sufficiently committed to the planting plans to lead the 'disruptive change' necessary, dealing with local objections to proposed plants as well as objections or confusion among diocesan staff and the various diocesan committees that need to understand and get behind the plans. When dioceses have set numerical goals for planting, it becomes clear that dedicated time and energy is required. We suggest that someone on the senior leadership team takes the role of 'sponsor' with overall responsibility for developing and delivering the planting plans. Additionally, it is wise to appoint a member of staff as a 'director', whose role is to undertake the detailed work needed to develop and deliver the plans. Finally, there might be a need for a programme manager to deal with necessary measurement, tracking and reporting to keep the project on track. I would suggest too that church planting is regularly on the senior leadership agenda and that it is undergirded with prayer.

Allocating resources strategically

Church planting and revitalisations at scale cost money and require training resources and management time. It is therefore vital to consider this at a local and diocesan-wide level. For resource churches, the treasurer should ensure there is a budget line for church planting. I know first-hand that a number of resource churches have sent significant sums of money, of the order of £50,000 per plant, as a gift, in addition to any strategic funds provided by the diocese or the national Church Strategic Development Funding. Incumbents make sure that money is put aside each year, so that when they come to plant, they are ready to give generously. As a recipient of this, I can tell you it makes a huge difference and is a wonderful act of sacrificial generosity by the sending church.

For dioceses, how can funds be set aside for planting to incentivise and enable church plants to happen, that otherwise couldn't without that funding? Could funds be raised from trusts or individuals that could be matched with

Make sure that sufficient resources are provided to meet the cost of the diocese's church-planting plans

money set aside by a diocese? It is prudent to make sure that sufficient resources are provided to meet the cost of the diocese's church-planting plans, both in the short and longer term. In practice, dioceses find this difficult because they would rather not reallocate resources from other activities, but we simply need to ask the question of what is going to give the better return and challenge the way the balance sheet is considered. Just because money hasn't been used for this purpose before, does not mean that funds cannot be released with creativity and faith.

Cost considerations might include the upfront costs needed for making buildings fit for purpose, for restructuring roles and for programme management. Additional stipendiary posts might be required above and beyond the current cohort of clergy for church planting. And different types of church plants might require a particular package of investment to help them succeed.

The relative state of church buildings is vital to consider. Almost every church revitalisation involves some kind of building project to make the church building fit for purpose. If you are expecting people to come in numbers, then meeting rooms, offices, kitchen facilities and toilets are pre-requisites. In addition, having flexible space in church naves usually means the removal of pews or at least movable pews, so that it can be used for weekday and evening ministries and events. Building projects should be activated as early as possible in the planting process. If a building project does not start until the plant is up and running it can easily swamp the leader and diverts mission energy. When these costs are factored in, they can enable direct mission costs, especially of staff, to be freed up for growing the church in its community.

Aligning your systems and support structures

After our first two plants in Shadwell, our treasurer Jacquie Driver, reorientated our budget around church planting and we realised that 40 per cent of our funds were going towards church planting activity, locally and nationally. We needed to align our vision, strategy, training, leadership development, evangelism and contextual mission around the planting activity that God was calling us to. Even though there were lean years, our congregation was more excited about giving to church plants than they were about keeping our own lights switched on!

For a diocese, working through ambitious planting goals and working with resource churches and church-planting churches, it is essential to ensure that its systems, policies and practices all fully support its church-planting plans. This will include:

- Curate deployment – it is reasonable to keep giving planting curates to resource churches because they are being trained for a specific purpose to revitalise churches and they will be sent with people and funding, which is unlikely with other church placements.

- Training for planting curates might be different to existing parish curacies because they will be involved in high-capacity change management situations, as well as bespoke ministry support. Some dioceses ae beginning to expect all their curates to be trained as church planters so they understand what is involved.

- Diocesan Directors of Ordinands must help to recruit future church planters, understanding the unique calling and gifts they require. Many dioceses have adjusted their policies to enable ordinands to stay in place after ordination so they can develop the necessary planting DNA and build the trust needed to take church members on their teams (see policy example in the Appendices).

- The parish share system[150] needs to support church planting rather than choking it. Some dioceses have formulae based on church attendance – the higher the number, the larger the amount needing to be given back to the diocese. In my view, this has consistently deterred and disincentivised church growth.

- Mission and Pastoral Committees should be structured to understand and seize missional opportunities as they arise, rather than getting them tied up in red tape or lost in committee meetings.

- The Diocesan Advisory Committee, responsible for developing church buildings, must be aligned to the vision for church planting. Problems have arisen where amenity societies have been more concerned with preserving the past than allowing buildings to be changed to enable increased levels of ministry activities. They are working together much more in many places, but alignment and early communication is essential to enable the buildings to be fit for purpose.

- Logistical support for church planting should be made available from central diocesan functions to support questions and issues around buildings, housing, HR, legal matters, safeguarding and communications.

Pulling it all together

If you've got to the end of this list, you have done well! The reason it is long and thorough is because diocesan structures are set up for maintaining the status quo. But church planting goes against the status quo, against the tide, and can sometimes hit a number of obstacles along the way. All I would say, is that if you pay attention to the areas in this chapter, and take a pragmatic, can-do approach to them, you are much more likely to have a smoother ride.

In the next chapter, we deal with developing the leaders who are going to lead resource churches and the church planters planting from them. They are the leaders of disruptive change, and they need to be well equipped in order to lead as effectively as possible.

ALL SAINTS WOODFORD WELLS

Diocese of Chelmsford

*All Saints Woodford Wells is a vibrant, charismatic evangelical Anglican church in the heart of Woodford Green in the London Borough of Redbridge. Within the Diocese of Chelmsford, it has a smaller sister church, and together they have planted or revitalised another five churches, which all now form All Saints' Minster. The leader, **Revd Paul Harcourt** (also National Director of the New Wine Network) says:*

I have been at All Saints Woodford Green for 25 years, first as curate for our sister church St Andrews and then as vicar of All Saints. We are a large suburban church, in the area where East London ends and Essex begins, and we have a mix of reasonably affluent people with some pockets of deprivation. Nearby, there are areas of more significant need, and so all our efforts in church planting and revitalisation have been into those areas. We have benefitted from our experience of partnering with St Andrews (a much smaller church half a mile away, which used to be the church for the servants of the parish) when working with the diocese to see how resources could be better used to support ministry in poorer areas.

We have long considered ourselves as a 'resourcing church'; we have had a specific vision since 2005 to 'go beyond ourselves' – to go beyond our own resources into God's and beyond our parish boundary into a regional responsibility. We were taken with the Scripture: 'From those to whom much has been given, much will be required' and we looked to play our part in a much bigger vision to see the revitalisation of East London. We started talking to the diocese about various opportunities. For example, we saw that we had more people in our congregation from the parish of Highams Park than were on the electoral role of that church, and so when the incumbent retired a few years later, our associate minster moved in and took a group of about 35 people with him, plus finance to support the changes. This saved the diocese valuable resources, and we made the sacrifice to lose our associate minister and the team, although to be honest this left a large hole (mainly in our sister church) which took a long time to rebuild.

However, being a resource church is an integral part of our DNA. We are very committed to the Bishop of Islington's church growth strategy, to the extent that our congregation is shown public domain maps, to see how our planting fits into a much larger strategic national vision. Our people know that the reason for our second curate is due to our willingness to invest in other churches, and that most of our curates will be taking part in future church revitalisations, where we will send a team to come alongside an existing congregation and bring new leadership. We send an injection of new people and finance, bringing them into part of a bigger team, and help them revitalise their Sunday worship and their sense of mission and local engagement. There is a sense that because we share the same values as the planting or revitalising team, the remaining congregation of the larger, better-resourced church, does not feel that it is giving away to strangers, but that we are all part of a bigger family. The closer relationship we can have between the sent team and the remaining congregation, the better the levels of trust and glad investment of money and prayer. Being a resourcing church means being trusted with precious additional resources, and the diocese should be able to see an existing kingdom vision (much as they would recognise an individual's call to ordination). In our case, we do not receive any extra finance, but we do get two title post curates rather than one, which is a significant investment of diocesan resources, and enables us to sustain a leadership pipeline.

In planting our five churches so far, we worked within the existing diocesan strategy, which mandated that churches work in groups as clergy numbers were reduced and so we worked out how we could do that while helping to resource and revitalise the work already going on in difficult places. We have good relationships now, but it was seen as quite threatening at the time, maybe due to our evangelical churchmanship which is unusual in our area. We needed to reassure people that we would work with them and honour what they knew and rebuild with it. We have had great support from Bishop Peter Hill, and now hopefully we have moved beyond any anxiety of a takeover to being seen as very positive and a beneficial resource to other churches and areas which would not otherwise be able to sustain any ministry.

Our plant into All Saints Highams Park was launched in 2012. We then took on St Cedd's Barkingside in 2016, when I was made Priest-in-Charge, and we appointed a fantastic lay worker (now curate) to run it. We co-opted St Paul's Hainault, who have their own incumbent but benefit from a resourcing and supportive relationship with us. Also, we have a Strategic Development Funded-church plant into a new housing estate at Barking Riverside which we oversee. We were responsible for identifying the lead planter and we sent a small team there from All Saints, using a model of self-replicating hubs of six which worked well in lockdown and was appropriate to the setting. Our most recent revitalisation is Holy Trinity South Woodford, which already had a clear identity and so this does mean significant change for them. We are being particularly slow and careful there, and we sent our curate, **Abi Todd**, who says:

Bishop Peter Hill asked me to consider taking on Holy Trinity South Woodford, revitalising it and bringing new life, while I was still a curate at

All Saints. Staying linked to All Saints was one of the factors that gave me confidence to move ahead with the idea. Holy Trinity was keen to have me, but initially not so keen on All Saints' involvement! However, planting in this way has made a huge difference. I attend All Saints' staff meetings, where I can share concerns, get ideas and be prayed for. I often ask for help from the All Saints' admin team, advice about weddings, even photocopying, as we have no formal admin function. And All Saints have been hugely generous, sending us with a large grant and then raising more money for us, even during lockdown. This has certainly turned some heads and hearts at Holy Trinity as they have begun to see what a church can look like when it is focused outwards – Holy Trinity is not there yet, but we have a vision of what can be in All Saints. I am really grateful to Paul and to be part of this model of church planting. We hope that in a few years we'll be planting too.

We now form a 'Mission and Ministry Unit' in our diocese's language – a group of churches working together under a framework or covenant. We have innovated a minster model, and our group of seven churches now forms the All Saints Minster, with a shared set of values. The leadership of all seven churches meet as one team every week, enabling the free flow of resources, ideas and mutual support. We may need to look at expanding the minster into two teams in future as we continue to grow.

In terms of raising and training young leaders, we are becoming more intentional with this, both using lay leaders and training them from within, and using clergy from the pipeline of curates who come to do a placement with us and then take a team to plant out from here. We are particularly focused on training in the areas of preaching and music, so we have big groups of lay people currently being trained in preaching and service leading and a pool of musicians who are being invested in, all with a view to future planting needs.

As I am National Leader of the New Wine network, we are also involved with the New Wine church planting development strategy (headed up by John McGinley), which identifies a number of church-planting hubs, of which All Saints is one. We offer our experience in planting to any churches who are interested, and we run church-planting training through the New Wine network as well as the diocese.

We believe that having a kingdom vision of church means that we should always see ourselves as a resourcing church. It's never enough to build ourselves up; we are always looking to extend, to go beyond ourselves into God's resources.

The Right Revd Peter Hill, Bishop of Barking

We are called in order to be sent! For me that is the practical heart of Christian discipleship and mission. The diversity of local context and opportunity means careful discernment and a mixed ecology in the way we set about our missional task. Today, church planting through resource churches is one effective means to that end.

My determination as bishop with oversight of church planting in the Diocese of Chelmsford, has been to develop a rolling programme of identifying and equipping resource churches. We have committed internal resourcing in terms of personnel, housing and funding, and have been strongly supported by the Church of England's Strategic Development Funding, in terms of methodology as well as significant external funding. The support and encouragement of the central Church of England's Strategy and Development Unit, and the counsel of the Bishop of Islington with his national church planting brief, have been essential to the task, as has the commitment of our own staff team.

Alongside diversity of tradition, our prayerful discernment has been around leadership, missional intention, generosity and multiplication. Those four key factors are biblical, overlapping and essential to the task.

Talent spotting such apostolic leaders, who understand the call to be sent, has been the starting point. They are those with strong initiating and entrepreneurial gifts, rather than those who emphasise sustaining their own parish church. They are willing risk-takers, eager for growth and impatient of others who do not see growth in numbers, discipleship and mission as a priority. They are sometimes impatient and demanding of me as a bishop, which is a good thing!

What characterises a resource church? It must be intentionally outward looking and willing to generously give itself away repeatedly. Its prayerful intention and energy must be focused on making disciples, as Jesus commanded, not just converts (Matt. 28:19), for true disciples make other disciples. A resource church is marked out by generosity in terms of disciples, leaders and money. It gives itself away sacrificially for the sake of Christ and the good news. In practical terms, that means a constant willingness to identify planting teams and commission leaders who it sends out to that new housing development, that declining parish church in need of resurrection, or that school hall or community centre in a strategic area for mission. We should not underestimate the sacrifice involved in terms of the mother church losing leaders and giving. But we so often see that generosity honoured by the Lord as new disciples and leaders take their place over time. It also means that the bishop and archdeacon have a responsibility to see such resource churches are continuously resourced themselves.

Resourcing resource churches with trainee leaders is paramount. To ensure multiplication continues, new planting leaders must be continually trained and sent out. As we progress our resource churches, we are committed to those new leaders being of both genders, lay or ordained and from diverse cultures, especially here in this large multicultural diocese.

Over the last two years, we have seen the benefit of monthly prayer gatherings sustaining our intention. Usually over lunch, they have provided opportunity for sharing, learning and support across plants. We are setting up a diocesan learning community for both planters and pioneers across the spectrum of new worshipping communities and social enterprise to enhance learning, share insights and nurture growth.

Church planting is a risky business, but we cannot be risk averse for the sake of the gospel. It demands faith, generous resourcing and flexibility; learning as we go along according to context. We will at times fail in planting and then it is best to recognise that reality early: in effect to fail fast, with support for leaders and recognition of alternatives. Several times, early on we have recognised we were on the wrong track and changed strategy or abandoned ship. Patience is required. In some contexts, growth is rapid, in others, the ground is hard and the leaders need extra support.

There has, as ever, been negative criticism and misgivings from those who take a different view on the need for church growth or simply feel they have been left out. National resourcing has prioritised urban areas, the disadvantaged and the young, so there has been understandable kickback from some in more rural contexts. The truth is that we can no longer rely on one model of church, namely the parish, if we want to see growth. It simply does not work well in certain contexts. Innovation attracts interest and buy-in, especially from younger Christian disciples and young outsiders who seek novelty in the way we extend the kingdom of God. And nobody can deny that we need to grow a younger church! Developing resource churches is demanding of energy and leadership on all concerned, but I am convinced it is worth it.

CHAPTER 8

DEVELOPING LEADERS FOR RESOURCE CHURCHES

Church leadership is critically important. There are many definitions and types of leadership but it is usually obvious when either effective or ineffective leadership is being exercised. The short-term impact is of things getting done well or not. The longer-term shows fruitfulness, especially in others, or passivity where little is growing, or worse, showing destruction and decline. We know from our Grow Course at the Gregory Centre, working with over 75 churches, that growth in churches is significantly helped or hindered by their church leaders.

Resource churches and their plants need highly competent leaders because they are in a position of significant responsibility. Different responsibilities are expected of them than with parish church leaders. They are not better, but they are different which is why attention should be paid to supporting them. They need to lead their church to grow in depth, in impact and in numbers. And they need to develop leaders who have the skills to lead the many groups and ministries that a growing church enables, as well as preparing leaders and teams to be sent to plant or revitalise other churches. Church planters developed and sent from resource churches have additional leadership expectations on them because of the start-up nature of their work and the huge change management and emotional intelligence involved in joining together a planting team with the receiving church and building and growing something new.

Church planters developed and sent from resource churches have additional leadership expectations on them

What kind of leaders are we talking about?

A resource church leader is called to create and grow a resource church to play its part in resourcing mission beyond their parish throughout a town or city, by planting and revitalising churches, developing leaders for mission, and working closely with their bishop. These skills are not taught in theological colleges and have so far only been picked up in a handful of churches that have done this before. As more resource churches are created the available pool of leaders is also growing in number and diversity.

There are dynamics of church size that need to be taken into account. Tim Keller's paper on Leadership and Church Size Dynamics[151] is a must-read for anyone wanting to get to grips with this. Essentially, Keller argues that different sizes of church require different leadership styles and practices. Smaller churches operate differently to larger churches in terms of how decisions are made, how much access there is to the leader, who does pastoral care and ministry of various kinds. Resource church leaders need to be comfortable with moving towards larger church leadership where ministry is about enabling and empowering others. It is often more managerial and less hands-on and not for everyone. Again, being a resource church leader is not better, it is just different, and those leaders need to understand what they should not spend their time on as much as what they should.

Resource church leaders need to be comfortable with moving towards larger church leadership where ministry is about enabling and empowering others

Resource church leaders also need to develop skilful church planters. They need to impart leadership in prayer, planning, envisioning, strategy, discipling, teaching, team building, prioritising and leadership development. Planters using these skills will need to navigate the challenges of a start-up, leading the transition into a more stable growing church, and then developing their own leaders for planting again. Alongside this, resource church leaders and their planters need to lead with humility among local church peers and nurture a good working relationship with their bishop.

These people don't grow on trees, but leaders can be developed for particular purposes and contexts if attention is paid to their growth in skills and character. We see this in the leadership advice from Jethro to Moses in Exodus 18:21 where leaders are to be selected for their capability, godliness and integrity, and in Paul's advice to Timothy in 2 Timothy 2:2 to pass on what he has learnt to reliable people who are qualified to teach others. Both point to skills and character as essential selection criteria.

The skills to lead larger, growing churches are usually nurtured in larger, growing churches where the dynamics of scale are learned and reflected on. That will include good preaching ability, particularly to congregations or groups of over 200 people, leadership skills, including the ability to recruit, train, deploy and motivate other leaders, the management and development of staff, vision formation and communication, and budget setting and keeping, on a different scale to the usual parish context.

Character in resource church leaders will have been refined and nurtured over many years. Leaders need to be prayerful and full of faith, expecting great things of God. They need to be able to live with the 'now' but lead people to the 'not yet.' They need to seek the kind of church where God is moving powerfully in people's lives. They will be generous in giving away ministry, training and releasing other leaders, seeking opportunities to plant and giving away their best people for the benefit of the kingdom of God. They will be humble, having a desire to learn from others and grow personally, able to submit to those in authority, and honouring other leaders in the city and the church. They will be collaborative, working in unity with other churches and their leaders, promoting teams and having fun along the way. And they will be resilient and tenacious, aware of leading healthily across a broader and more complex canvas.

Leadership development within resource churches

Developing leaders in resource churches increases the church's capacity to grow and send planting teams. If a church leader insists on leading everything themselves, the church will not grow very much. But if the leader gives away responsibility, enabling other leaders to emerge, then growth naturally follows as they are encouraged and developed to gather people and teams, giving them focus and direction. By focusing on leadership development, there will be more than enough leaders to send on church plants and space for new leaders to grow within the sending church. I want to look at three stages: recruiting, developing and sending.

If the leader gives away responsibility, enabling other leaders to emerge, then growth naturally follows

1. Recruiting leaders

I have had the privilege of being recruited and trained by some extraordinary leaders. Evangelist J John recruited me to be his assistant, carrying his bags and driving his car. He taught me and trained me and entrusted me with increasing responsibility so that I grew in confidence and competence. I was recruited by Unilever as a marketing manager and was thrown into the deep end, with good supervision and training on-the-job. Nicky Gumbel, then a curate at Holy Trinity Brompton (HTB), recruited me to be a pastoral assistant and gave me opportunities to lead and learn about creating leadership teams and giving people the chance to develop their gifts. The vicar of HTB, Sandy Millar, invited me to be a worship leader there where I learned about developing worship and teams on a wider canvas. After ordination training, Sandy invited me back to be a curate at HTB and gave me increasing responsibility and opportunity to lead. Over my time at HTB, Sandy invested in me one-to-one weekly for over 12 years before sending us to lead a church plant in East London.

I have seen that the best place to recruit planting leaders is from within the resource church. They have lived with the vision and embraced the church's culture. Leaders get to see emerging leaders in action and can nurture their growth and development. It is good then to cultivate an expectation of spotting and inviting people into taking leadership responsibility throughout the church. When they do well with a little, then they can be entrusted with more. I have come to appreciate those who are really good at spotting leaders as well. They are like gifted headhunters within churches, and when you find those people, I encourage you to draw them in to further nurture the latent talent that is already in your midst.

Leaders get to see emerging leaders in action and can nurture their growth and development

But recruit wisely! It is easy to invite someone into leadership, but it is much harder to remove them if it doesn't work. Be careful who you choose and remember Paul's words to Timothy, 'Do not be hasty in the laying on of hands' (1 Tim. 5:22). I keep going back to the tried and tested 5 Cs for assessing potential leaders, especially for planting:

- Competence – will they be good at what they need to do in a church plant?
- Chemistry – are they good at building healthy team dynamics?
- Character – are they teachable and being refined by Christ?
- Culture – do they embody the vision and values of the church?
- Calling – are they called to be a planter, innovator or pioneer?

New churches need leaders who are fit for purpose; gifted and equipped to face the enormous challenges that church planting involves. The best place for church planters to learn about planting is in a church plant, especially in the first year of a plant, where they can learn as it happens, or in a church-planting church, where it is intrinsically part of the culture and practice. Curates allocated to church plants as curates to the main planter should act as assistants, ready to shoulder responsibility and add value from day one, while learning on the job. Dioceses, therefore, should look to resource churches and church-planting churches for their pipeline of future leaders of church plants. Lead planters should therefore have been given experience of managing staff already, so it is not a new skill for them. Churches that understand this will often have their own patterns of developing leaders, and they can be encouraged to invest further in this by bishops and senior teams. To widen the net, bishops can work proactively with theological colleges, who are increasingly recognising the need to identify church planting as one of their training options.[152]

Bishops can also actively source planters from diocesan intern schemes. These younger leaders learn quickly and are already open to being thrown into situations where they will be stretched and developed further. Examples of using these schemes for recruiting planters include Leeds Diocese partnering with and expanding the intern programme at St George's Leeds;[153] Southwell Diocese creating a Younger Leadership College to inspire and commission a thousand younger leaders;[154] and the same diocese using an intern programme with eight young people living in community at a strategic planting location. Of course, lay planters should also be encouraged, noting the fresh expressions data that 40 per cent of Fresh Expressions are led by untrained lay people.[155] As a church planter, I would want some of these lay planters on my team!

Bishops should also be proactive about seeking planters from a wide range of ethnic and social backgrounds. This is essential for many reasons, not least the biblical understanding of the equality of all peoples and valuing the richness that comes with racial and ethnic diversity. This is an ongoing challenge in the Church of England.[156] A recent initiative from HTB and St Mellitus College, called 'The Peter Stream,' encourages people from different backgrounds who would not necessarily see themselves as candidates for ordination to find a welcoming training pathway.[157] This fast-growing vocational track is enabling people from different ethnicities and socio-economic backgrounds to get involved in church planting and church leadership in general.[158] We must recognise our own unconscious bias and make a conscious change to recruit more diversely and we must allow ourselves to be shaped by the kind of leaders that God is sending us, rather than shaping them into our existing models.

We must allow ourselves to be shaped by the kind of leaders that God is sending us, rather than shaping them into our existing models

2. Developing leaders

Once leaders have been identified, give them every opportunity to grow and develop as a leader in hands-on situations. As you see them in action, proactively give them feedback and chances to hone their skills. You might want to put them on external leadership courses or develop your own programme to prepare them as well as possible to be effective in their leadership.

I think the best way to develop leaders is to create an apprentice culture where every leader in the church has an apprentice. That means the senior leader trains their planting curate as an apprentice; the children's church leader apprentices other children's leaders; an Alpha group leader has an Alpha helper as an apprentice. Learning from the craft guilds movement,[159] an apprentice learns all the tools of the trade, including passing that trade on to others. We should encourage our apprentices not just to learn from us, but to learn how to pass it on to others too.

The diocesan Director of Ordinands and those responsible for training in a diocese must ensure planting curates get the best kind of training to do what they are going to do. They are planting churches from scratch, taking and leading a team with them, and handling complex change management issues. Directors of Training will need to adapt their training curriculum so as not to overload planting curates with too much input.

Training is essential, and knowledge and experience should not be assumed. Sending churches should work through what training they can offer. Church-planting modules should be offered to ordinands in their training. Planting curates should be allocated to planting churches and trained there for church planting. In the year approaching the launch of the plant, the focus of their attention will shift to where they are going and the training they will need. Networks experienced in planting have their own bespoke training, such as HTB's Accelerator Course and New Wine's Planting Cohorts. And I encourage planters to shape their strategy and detailed planning using carefully designed and tested tools such as those developed on the Gregory Centre Plant Course,[160] alongside galvanising prayer, to make sure they are as prepared as they can be.

3. Sending leaders

Once the location and timing for a church plant have been decided, the next stage is sending. Without getting contractual, having an open and honest relationship between the sender and the planter in the sending stage is vital. Issues that need to be addressed in advance include expectations around the size of the team being sent, who can be invited and how, when announcements will be made, how much money is being given and what responsibilities can be passed on to enable space to plan and prepare.

It is good practice to ask the sending church leader for permission to have conversations with particular people so that decisions being made are out in the open. If the planter invites key leaders and givers without careful consideration to the impact on the sending church and who will replace them, it can damage trust and undermine generosity. On the other hand, sending church leaders are marked by being generous and sacrificial, giving some of their best leaders away. For some, they might even be called to go with the team, having ensured that all of their responsibilities, skills and expertise have been passed on well. However it is done, and whoever goes, good internal communication is critical to a successful planting process.

The resource church leader should ensure the planter has a coach, to help them work through the questions and issues that need to be faced, and the support they will need to be effective. The one-on-one time that I had with Sandy Millar equipped me not just with formation in skills and character, but with the emotional and spiritual support I needed to believe I could do it. He prayed for me, encouraged me, challenged me and stood by me. It made all the difference. Give planters everything possible to succeed.

Once the planter has been sent, I think it is good to continue the connection in a relational way with the sending church. In Tower Hamlets, we established a local network where the planted churches met together, learned together and prayed together. It did not undermine deanery or diocesan structures but strengthened us in the pursuit of excellence in our collective mission. We met not because we had to but because we wanted to. I always encourage planters to be part of a network that will equip and help them to be the best possible leaders they can be. When bishops encourage these relational, horizontal networks, there is no threat to existing structures which are more hierarchical and vertical, rather the whole is strengthened and enhanced.

Building leadership capacity

One of the fears of larger churches is that church planting will take away some of the most active and gifted leaders, leaving the sending church in a mess and potentially a decline. This thinking needs to be reframed with a generosity mindset. We should try to give away our best leaders so that the plant is successful. And in order to do that, we need to be constantly developing leaders ready to be sent and ready to replace those who are sent. I remember learning this the hard way. One of the church plants at HTB went with 25 per cent of our leaders. HTB grew to replace the numbers sent after a few months, but it took two years to train up and replace the leaders who left. The good thing was that it created space for people to grow, but we were not prepared for it. It had to become a priority.

To build leadership capacity well takes focused attention. I have found the leadership pipeline model so helpful in addressing this.[161] In mid-sized and larger churches there are five stages in the pipeline (see figure 11):

1. Leading self – members of the church.

2. Leading others – small group leaders, children's church leaders, etc.

3. Leading teams – ministry oversight leaders.

4. Leading leaders – curates or senior lay leaders, congregation leaders.

5. Leading networks – the senior leader of the church.

From a leadership point of view, we want everyone to lead themselves, taking responsibility for developing their character, their skills, their devotional life, their own discipleship, their financial giving and beginning to encourage and disciple others. Where we see leadership potential, we want to encourage and develop that so that it can be exercised in every part of the church. The first opportunity to lead might be in an Alpha group, a Bible study group, a children's church group or a small serving team. Leading larger teams and ministries will involve leading people who are leading others. This calls for different skills and a greater expectation on godly character. Leading groups of ministries and leading an overall church with networks of leaders requires different leadership again.

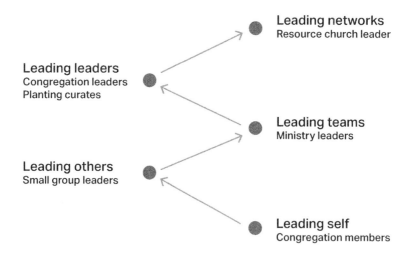

Figure 11. A church leadership pipeline.

This tool is useful in many ways. It helps leaders understand what skills are required of them at each level. It informs what kind of training is needed. It demonstrates that it is essential to develop character early on because when leadership goes wrong it has such an impact on those following. It also helps identify people who are ready to grow in leadership and take on new responsibility, progressing through the pipeline. At the same time, it is important not to progress too quickly without learning the essential skills and developing the character appropriate to that level of leadership responsibility.

Using a leadership pipeline increases the capacity of leaders in the church. As I said earlier, I encourage every leader to have an apprentice. Then there is always someone ready to start a new group to increase the capacity of that ministry in the church. It also means there is capacity to send a leader on a church plant or replace a leader who is sent. If everyone is in a small group of, say, 10 people with a leader and an apprentice leader, that means there should be a minimum of 20 per cent of the church being trained in leadership. If you factor in a desire to grow the church and have capacity to plant as well, there may be as many as 40 per cent being actively trained in some way. Intentionally growing a leadership pipeline in this way will need careful and timely attention.

Sending out planting teams

I have seen over the years that if a church planter goes alone to plant, it is hard in many ways. But if a team accompanies them, the load is spread, more gifts and skills can be used, more is achieved, change happens more quickly, and it is more fun. The resource church should plan to send a team that is appropriate to the size of the context they are going to. Some situations need a large team, so that momentum is achieved; others require smaller teams that won't overwhelm the place they are going. Either way, teams make a difference.

With a pipeline of leaders, a sending church can be confident in sending a planting team that has built-in future leadership capacity. A planting curate can plan to take leaders who can take responsibility for any ministries that are needed from day one of the plant – perhaps Alpha leaders, children or youth workers, or compassion ministry leaders, and people to look after the organisational and administrative side of church, including the finances and governance. While the planting curate is responsible overall, many can be involved and play their part, releasing much more ministry right from the beginning.

Many can be involved and play their part, releasing much more ministry right from the beginning

Church planters should invite their team to commit to the process for a minimum length of time – in our planting it was for at least a year. I have further broken that down into five elements of commitment because it helps the team know what is involved:

1. Belonging – to the new church as a wholehearted member.

2. Serving – on a team to enable the church to be as effective as it can be.

3. Giving – financially to the church, sacrificially and regularly.

4. Praying – for the church, its vision and for its leaders.

5. Discipling – others by helping them grow in their faith.

One subset of discipling others is nurturing emerging leaders as apprentices, honing skills and character as above, and so the beginnings of a leadership pipeline can be part of the sending team from the beginning too.

Planning for multiplication

So, once a resource church has been designated, it should plan for the multiplication of planters and teams from the outset. When we planted in East London, I preached on the first Sunday about the need to plant again. We recruited a planting curate and planned and prayed for planting. What we hadn't anticipated was that there would be two planting opportunities rather than just one. We prayed and discussed it and decided to do both within a week of each other. It stretched our faith and our structures, but God provided all we needed, and it became such a blessing to us to see two churches come to life again. And within a year, we had grown by 25 per cent of our pre-planting numbers. We experienced the faithfulness of God and we were determined to structure ourselves to be able to do it again and again.

TRINITY CHURCH NOTTINGHAM
Diocese of Southwell and Nottingham

*Trinity Church Nottingham began when the Diocese of Southwell and Nottingham invited Holy Trinity Brompton (HTB) to plant a city-centre resourcing church. Bishop Paul Williams identified a need and invited a small team comprised of the leaders, **Revd Jonny and Amy Hughes**, and a curate, Revd Will Foulger, with one other staff member and three interns. After beginning to gather in homes from September 2016, Trinity Church held its first public service at Easter 2017, and now meets in the former Neale's Auction House on Mansfield Road, acquired by the diocese. Jonny writes:*

The team, which was gathered from HTB, our sending church, as well as through other relationships, was small and relatively inexperienced. We took note of this in the process of our planting, as we deliberately took our time in a gradual way, slowly working out the skills of the team and what the vision was. The name, Trinity Church Nottingham, was partly inspired by hearing the story of nearby Holy Trinity Church, which had existed in what is now Trinity Square, and had contributed for 100 years to education and church planting before the building was demolished in 1957 to make room for a car park. We felt we were being involved in a resurrection project. The most extraordinary facet of our early months was discovering that a Nottingham-based man had had a dream that the derelict building into which we moved was to be a church, a full four years before our arrival. Shortly after having the dream, he began to pray for the building, doing so weekly on a Sunday for a period of more than two years before our arrival. None of us knew anything of this until our first service on Easter Sunday 2017. Naturally, hearing of it filled us with confidence of God's presence with us.

We have grown from eight people meeting to pray in our front room to around 400 people, including 50 children. We are a disproportionately young church, with lots of people in their 20s and 30s, although we do have a good range of every decade after that and some folk in their 80s. We are becoming increasingly diverse, and although we are an attractional, gathered church, we are based in an area which is close to many areas of deprivation. We are now having more local people join us, and we are growing community groups such as our Trinity Tots group, giving more space for local people and meeting a need – this gained momentum before the Covid-19 pandemic. We are partnering with Safe Families, a charity which supports families to avoid children being taken into care, and we anticipate seeing this partnership grow. We took part in

Love Your Neighbour during lockdown which worked well for us, and our sense of community involvement and social engagement is beginning to grow as we become more experienced.

We have been very fortunate to have the support of a great diocesan senior team and an incredibly supportive bishop. One of our strengths is our capacity to raise up leaders and help people move into vocations. We have a number of young ordinands on our team, a couple of curates, and at least another 10 young people who are on the journey towards ordination. It wasn't a deliberate policy, but this has happened organically as we spend a lot of time investing in young people, both formally and informally. We are also signed up to the diocesan Apprentice Track, which is a year-long internship based around a life of apprenticeship to Jesus. We have found that this can act as a more formal leadership pipeline, as people who are early on in their discernment process can be placed in the church for their internship, and can spend time marinating in our culture before moving on to ordination. The Apprentice Track started around the same time as Trinity Church, and we have enjoyed being able to help shape it and support the initiative rather than invent our own. It's working really well so far.

We also have the gift of being the host church for the East Midlands campus for St Mellitus Theological College. This fits in well with our wider vision to see Trinity Church become something akin to an urban monastery, in which learning and sending sit alongside prayer, worship, and hospitality. They have an office in our building and do regular teaching sessions for years one and two of their course. We love hosting them and facilitating this, and we are seeing people come into leadership from non-denominational backgrounds as well as through a traditional Church of England route.

We were established as a resource church from the start, and the diocese has always used that language – it certainly fits with our vision to give ourselves away, and there is an expectation that we will be planting new worshipping communities and campuses in the near future. We are currently working with a hugely visionary and capable bishop and diocese, and so we are more than happy to work within their vision for church planting and disciple-making and it is a great partnership in that sense.

We are beginning work on a new worshipping community in Hockley near the Lace Market, simply beginning with a series of prayer meetings to discern what God is doing. Beyond that, we anticipate a number of new opportunities in the next few years. The limiting factor at this stage is the number of ready leaders, and so once we have more leaders ordained in the next three to five years, we hope to see exponential growth in Nottingham.

Looking back, we are glad we have not rushed the planting or the growth of

Trinity Church – we have not seen it as a franchise operation, but have looked at what we had the team and expertise to do, what God was saying, and what was needed at that particular time. While we may not have done anything hugely innovative or unique, God has led our steady and quiet growth and more people are joining the story every week. We believe that the same God who was at work generations ago in the original Holy Trinity Church is at work now in us, and we feel called to continuing in the path laid down for us.

The Rt Revd Paul Williams, Bishop of Southwell and Nottingham

As I had previously led a larger resourcing church and seen the benefits of such churches in the Diocese of London, and others in the senior diocesan team had experience of the concept, we considered resource churches to be a key engine in the implementation of the vision to grow disciples wider, younger, and deeper. While we value slow incremental growth in local church communities, in order to stem the decline and to turn that around into growth, a new engagement was required with focused vision and energy.

The aim of designating churches as resourcing churches was to enable them to become a beacon in mission and ministry, with clear and ambitious missional expectation, to develop expertise in a particular aspect of mission and ministry, to focus energy and resource on trying new approaches, and leading in innovative ways.

Resourcing churches are encouraged to develop a culture that grows in order to give itself away. This is a culture that we hope will spread throughout the diocese, leading to new worshipping communities developing in diverse contexts. In order to accelerate this process, key churches were needed to pioneer this commitment. Part of the diocesan vision launched in 2016 was to develop 25 churches who have the potential to become larger resourcing churches (greater than 250), scattered throughout the diocese, serving in the varied contexts that are here – urban, suburban, post-industrial, market town, and rural.

Trinity Church was the first new church designated as a resourcing church in the diocese, and to date, we have a cohort of 25 churches who are part of a learning community and working towards this goal. They represent these diverse contexts and also a variety of church traditions.

One challenge is the training and culture setting of the potential leaders of resourcing churches. Our learning community of 25 includes leaders at different stages of ministry and engagement with the resourcing church framework. Many are also leading local parish ministry while working towards the stretch of developing into a resourcing church. The learning community has enabled teaching and training around the values and shift of thinking that is needed to develop the culture and key aspects of leading a larger resourcing church. This is an ongoing journey and we are all learners.

There have been many encouragements. We have seen new worshipping communities planted from resourcing churches – one has two further plants in the pipeline; an increase in vocations from those churches and an increase in lay engagement and leadership training. One very welcome and unexpected outcome has been a substantial increase in people from more diverse ethnicities. We are in the process of developing the strategy around 'beacon' centres – hubs of excellence for children and youth ministry.

Trinity Church has had a significant impact in terms of numbers and has grown relatively rapidly, contributing to training events in the diocese, and is especially a beacon for worship leading, prayer and evangelism on the streets, and creative communication to younger cultures. The leadership at Trinity Church has fostered good relationships with already existing potential resource churches.

Other exciting communities have emerged. Woven – a group of revitalised churches working together under one vision in estates across north Nottingham – has been highly effective in youth work and mission to urban priority areas and is developing an innovative way of working. The Potting Shed Church has established a new worshipping community in a rural area, with a focus on creativity and community, especially with all-age worship and spiritual nurture, as well as being a resource to local rural churches. St Luke's Gamston – also part of the 25 – has planted a new worshipping community into a school and is planning a further two plants over the next two years, as well as resourcing a revitalisation in a local parish.

Ideally, resourcing churches become a catalyst for growth and change in a variety of contexts that helps with the inspiration and aspiration for other local churches. Resourcing churches are not only for city-centre settings but can thrive and grow in a range of contexts. If this is the case, it helps local churches in those areas to aspire to growth and disciple-making, and to achieve their missional objectives by sharing learning and resources for ministry and training. One final significant encouragement is the way some smaller churches have enthusiastically embraced the aspirations of larger resourcing churches, with a fresh commitment to enhance worship, revitalise children's ministry and plant new worshipping communities.

CHAPTER 9

OBJECTIONS AND OBSTACLES

When something new is introduced into an institution like the Church of England, it will raise questions and highlight challenges. Objections and obstacles in the Church are important to address because they can uncover bad theology, unhelpful models and unhealthy practices. They can also sharpen the arguments in favour of the change. The Church at large is very good at bringing these to our attention and it is often difficult to have a healthy debate. Here, I want to address objections as openly as I can and then look at the common change barriers in the creation of resource churches.[162] Firstly, these are the most common objections I have come across.

What is the theology behind resource churches?

I have addressed the theology of resource churches in Chapter 3 in more detail. However, I recognise that this is only really brushing the surface and there is so much more to uncover. I hope this book goes someway to opening up the debate and inviting a deeper engagement, especially with the theology and ecclesiology of resource churches. The theological basis of *any* church is beautiful, deep and multifaceted. It will include gathering disciples together to worship God, to fellowship with one another and to encourage each other to witness to the world, experiencing in different ways the sacramental life of the church, before being sent out to live that life in the community. Resource churches are usually parish churches that have been tasked by their bishop with helping other churches to thrive, in various ways, by growing and sending people and resources to strengthen that aim. Whether they 'do church' any differently depends on the theological emphasis of a particular church tradition and the missiology that arises from that.

The theological basis of any church is beautiful, deep and multifaceted

What about the impact on other church traditions?

This question is usually not spoken but it is nearly always close to the surface. It can be sensitive because different church traditions do sometimes feel threatened by one another. The Church of England has a rich tradition of both catholic and evangelical streams running through its historical veins. And there have always been liberalising movements that challenge and question the Church's engagement with the world. All of these traditions have waxed and waned over the centuries, sometimes with bitter and tragic consequences. Too often they feel threatened by one another and yet, seen in a different light, we need each one. I love the *Renovaré* movement, founded by author and speaker Richard Foster, that encourages the view that we need every tradition to truly envision a balanced spiritual life.[163]

We need every tradition to truly envision a balanced spiritual life

But what does this balance look like in practice? And should that question dominate the status quo at the expense of the church's growth or decline? In practical terms, if a particular church is struggling, independent of its tradition, I would suggest that an intervention of some kind is important. Does the priest need a break? Or a change? Research has shown that if a priest stays too long in a parish it can lead to serious decline.[164] Sometimes there is toxicity among church members that disables the church from its primary mission. In these cases, change is necessary, whether it is a change of leadership, a longer vacancy, an interim ministry or a revitalisation.

That change is usually seen as requiring a change of leadership, keeping the tradition the same. Though it is rarely articulated, I suppose this is to honour the existing tradition and not introduce too much change to the patterns that have existed for many years, though I do not see a theological reason for maintaining one particular tradition over and above another. The church PCC and its representatives are likely to articulate what they want in new leadership is someone to keep their tradition alive. That is well and good. But sometimes I think that this can inhibit something new and imaginative from happening that comes with a complete change.

If there is a change in tradition, much sensitivity and honouring of the past is required. Some churches have switched back and forth between traditions over the decades which can often be forgotten in the shorter term.[165] And some revitalisations have developed models of retaining former church traditions while introducing new ones.[166] Perhaps what is most important, is to bring the discussion out into the public space and articulate our hopes and fears in this area so we can listen and respond face to face rather than behind closed doors and people's backs.

Ultimately, we need every tradition to reach all peoples because the gospel is multifaceted, and each tradition reflects different elements of that gospel. Thus, when we stand shoulder to shoulder, facing the mission field, and the many who come nowhere near a church, we see the need not to dilute or diminish one tradition in favour of another, but the need for every tradition to engage in this mission.

The cathedral is a diocese's resource church – why do we need another?

What is the difference between a cathedral and a resource church? Well in one sense, both cathedrals and resource churches are called to resource other churches, but they do it in completely different ways. Cathedrals play a key role as the ecclesiastical and civic centre of a diocese's life. They are the seat of the bishop. Many cathedrals develop particular expertise that is given away to the wider church to build it up. Resource churches also tend to develop resources that can be given away, as *Cathedrals and resource churches should be complementary* other churches might, but they primarily resource a diocese by revitalising parishes and planting churches. Cathedrals and resource churches should be complementary and the more churches that are geared towards giving away what God has given them, the more the wider Church will thrive.

Are resource churches dismantling the parish system?

Parishes are created to enable every person in the land to have a parish church to which they can belong. William Temple famously said that the Church of England exists for the sake of its non-members.[167] Currently Anglican churches reach 1.2 per cent of the population. Resource churches are beginning to buck this statistic, especially attracting people who the Church is not currently reaching. While resource churches might draw members from an area beyond their parish boundaries, they are not alone in this. Many parish churches, especially in city and town centres, have members who choose their churches based on preference rather than geography. But in time, once they start planting and revitalising churches, resource churches actually begin to strengthen local churches in local areas because they are geared towards reaching new people in new places. This revalues why parishes were set up in the first place.

Larger churches dominate smaller churches – why are we favouring them?

I believe that every town and city, deanery or diocese, needs a mixture of different kinds of churches to reach different kinds of people. Larger churches can develop broad programmes and reach wide areas. Smaller churches can invest in smaller neighbourhoods and be more locally contextual. An area needs every kind of church, not just one kind. But it is never right when one church dominates another. I have seen churches that think they are 'doing better' because they happen to be larger and attract more people. Numerical size is not the only measurement and takes no account of unhealthiness. I have also seen churches that are even jealous of another's 'success,' rationalising their own unhealthiness and demonising the other's differences. Jesus calls us to love one another and that must include churches. We can appreciate difference as a good thing missionally without feeling threatened, and we can pray for one another and encourage one another towards love and good deeds.[168]

Each church is called to play its part in an area and in the kingdom of God. If part of that calling is to resource other churches, then two good reasons for investing in that church are to help them to do it more effectively and to help them to do it more often. That investment might feel like favouritism but it is a wise investment for a diocese. It will save money in the medium term as a church is revitalised and begins to increase its missional footprint in a new area, support its own costs rather than needing to be supported by the Common Fund, and even be in a position to support other churches in time.

Some have said that having a new vibrant church planted like this will drain the life of a dozen healthy but fragile churches nearby. Obviously, sensitivity is needed in every situation, but change should not be off the table. The issue of people transferring to new churches will always be a problem, whether they move to a church in a different denomination or because they have a specific need, such as for a youth group. I have found that when plans for a church plant are communicated among local churches in advance, those transfers can be a positive move where people are sent rather than just leave.[169] In some cases, local churches 'up their game,' taking advantage of the new missional energy in an area.[170]

Not many churches intentionally and actively give away members and significant finances to other churches

What is often missed are the huge sacrifices paid by church-planting and revitalising churches. Not many churches intentionally and actively give away members and significant finances to other churches. Yet this is regarded as a calling of resource churches and other church-planting churches. For a bishop to invest in churches like these so they can repeatedly do this sacrificial work is not favouring one church over another, but rather using these churches to reverse decline in other parts of the diocese.

One further point within this objection is the feeling of a takeover. This might be expressed as, 'It feels like this church is taking over and I don't like it.' Some statistics are worth highlighting here. There are 100 resource churches in the country, making up less than 0.8 per cent of parish churches. They are actually very small in number, even though they have a significant part to play. I have heard the same said of Holy Trinity Brompton (HTB) and its network of planted churches. By the end of 2020, HTB had planted or revitalised 18 resource churches and 16 other parish churches, and there are some 57 churches in its informal network, many of which are plants of plants. As a single church, I don't think that any other Church of England parish has given away as many people and as much money for mission as HTB has. With less than 0.5 per cent of Church of England parishes, it is amazing how many column inches of comment they generate. It is not so much a takeover, as an extraordinary outpouring of missional generosity.

Who holds the power?

There is a question of justice that is important to address. There are always power dynamics involved in churches, including church planting and parish revitalisations. The issues cluster around a vulnerable parish being revitalised by a well-resourced, more powerful, incoming church team. I had a very helpful conversation with Sam Wells, vicar of St Martin-in-the-Fields, about this when they were considering becoming a resource church at the invitation of the Bishop of London. He wanted to be clear that St Martin's and the HeartEdge network of churches were concerned about the power dynamics of this approach, preferring to come alongside to encourage and share rather than take over and dominate. They are now a resource church and I explain a little more about them in Chapter 10.

I think it is important to differentiate between the need for change and how that change is carried out. People will disagree about the need for change and there are many factors surrounding this. Following a significant local review in 2004, the Tower Hamlets deanery suggested that St Paul's Shadwell be closed because there were three other small Anglican churches nearby. This was against the church's wishes and something the Bishop of London disagreed with, which led to an invitation for us to plant there. There were numerous complex issues at play. Some changes are necessary whether it is closure, a change of missional emphasis or healing broken relationships from a previous incumbency. This is ultimately an episcopal decision and requires courage, discernment and wisdom.

How this change is then carried out is also critically important and goes to the heart of how we love one another. I was struck by Mark Jobe's revitalisation approach in New Life Community Church in Chicago.[171] He talked about 'honouring the past, navigating change in the present and building for the future.' Revitalisations are often needed when a parish is really struggling and where there needs to be a partnership between the original congregation and the incoming team. This can be done well or badly. The incoming team must come with great humility and prayerfulness, yet also with a bold ambition and tenacity for change. This needs much love, forbearance and grace, but has all the potential for huge transformation and blessing. After all, is this not the gospel outworked in the life of a local church? So, I stand by the need for revitalisations, but emphasise even more stronglr the need to do this with great sensitivity and love.

Why is a resource church being treated differently to us?

This objection arises when decisions seem to be fast-tracked when a resource church is created compared to the experience of regular churches. Some might feel that they have been given a planting curate, funding or permission to change their buildings more easily than others. It seems unfair. There are two responses worth considering here.

Firstly, many of these decisions happen relatively quickly because there are deadlines, often associated with funding, vacancy timings and the availability of particular buildings. In order to enable the whole project to work, they happen concurrently and so have a high impact on any observers.

But secondly, we should reframe the notion of fairness. There are examples in Scripture where fairness is called into question, like the parables of the workers in the vineyard (Matt. 20:1–16) and the parable of the bags of gold (Matt. 25:14–30). Everyone is not always treated the same. But fairness is not the same as justice. *It is sometimes easier to give everyone the same, but it is not necessarily wise or just* The Church is called to be just. So, when it comes to limited resources, the Church is faced with a choice of distributing its resources equally, and therefore thinly, or placing its resources in areas that will make a strategic difference. It is sometimes easier to give everyone the same, but it is not necessarily wise or just. It will of course feel different, depending on whether you are on the receiving end or not. An honest explanation of the wider diocesan strategy will go a long way to helping this.

Why are you giving extra money to resource churches? It's unfair!

A number of resource churches have been given funding as they are created, to put towards the costs of set up and up-front staffing. This funding has been a combination of Strategic Development Funding (SDF) and matched diocesan funding. Some have asked why this funding has been given to these churches and not distributed to others. Sometimes it might be expressed as, 'If you gave us £1M, our church would grow too.' Some have further criticised the whole SDF programme, questioning the distribution of many millions of pounds.

I think there are three responses to this. Firstly, the diocese has almost certainly made a strategic decision to invest in a few churches rather than every church equally. Investing in city-centre churches is important because of years of relative under-investment in England's urban centres. This means that some churches will receive investment and others will not. The amount of funding is secondary to this. It is not about being unfair but about stewarding limited resources wisely. Secondly, the strategic decision to invest in a resource church is made because it is appointed to revitalise other churches. This investment will pay back dividends in the future as churches are renewed. Thirdly, funding up front enables the church to be in a position to revitalise and plant earlier than if it had to develop this funding base on its own.

The strategic decision to invest in a resource church is made because it is appointed to revitalise other churches

It could have been handled better

I have seen a number of blog posts about resource churches that express where there are feelings of hurt and upset at something precious being lost. Some say they can see why a bishop might have decided to make the change, but they object to the way it has been carried out. There have been many mistakes in this area, and it is important not to brush these under the carpet. We must acknowledge these mistakes so that we can learn from them, apologise where appropriate, adapt as necessary and move on. Change often disrupts, but it can still be handled with care.

If someone hears about a significant change to the status quo of a church second or third hand, it can be painful and sometimes destructive. Even if done well, it can be hard if this is a different direction to what might have previously been envisaged. If, on the other hand, a decision or change were to be widely spoken about in advance, there might be a collective move to close ranks and protect the church against any change at all. Each situation requires sensitivity, but what is essential is good communication throughout the change process. It is easy to get this wrong and we have developed a simple stakeholder engagement tool to help with this (see Appendices). Handling a process badly is not an argument for *not* making a change. It is an argument for better planning and clear, consistent communication.

Obstacles to the creation of resource churches

If these objections are being voiced in public or behind closed doors from those raising legitimate questions about resource churches, in addition there are a number of obstacles that need to be navigated for those who are trying to create them. My own research has identified a specific list of barriers that bishops and their senior teams have encountered in real ways that need to be considered and overcome.

Resistance to change

Change can be difficult for many people. It will manifest in fear, jealousy, misunderstandings or institutional inertia and can be very deeply felt. It might be expressed by small churches fearing the impact of a resource church near them, 'taking their members away,' or of bigger churches, who are jealous of the attention that a new church is getting. It can be particular church traditions fearing a takeover or unfair favour. These deeply held views can block change for the better. Added to this, some church structures present issues simply because it is not what is 'normally done'.

Most waves of ecclesiastical innovation over the centuries were hotly resisted

Resistance to change is not a new thing! Most waves of ecclesiastical innovation over the centuries were hotly resisted. New church buildings, like chapels and chantries, were resisted by local clergy as attendance shifted to churches closer to where people lived.[172] Bishops who renewed and revitalised their dioceses were sometimes resisted by local leaders.[173] New churches proposed in the 19th century by Bishop Blomfield were roundly criticised as too ambitious.[174]

There is no easy way around this other than to acknowledge it and take it into account. Good communication, including good explanations and good listening, helps change. But perhaps what most trumps resistance to change is good leadership. Senior leaders need to take responsibility for the decision to create a resource church. This will involve owning that decision, giving clear direction and making the case for change, and patiently and personally addressing stakeholders in turn. This increases unity and builds a stronger vision. I have seen this delegated because of the fear of looking bad or not being liked and this makes the change process 10 times worse.

Personnel issues

Recruiting resource church leaders and planting curates can be an issue because existing structures might miss the best candidates. I have recruited a Resource and Relationship manager into the Islington team with independent funding to meet this need. Flexibility is key as these needs are simply not catered for in our current structures. It is easy not just to miss the best people but also to appoint the wrong people. Some people might be attracted to church planting because it sounds exciting, but they might not be at all suited to it. Leeds Diocese developed a very helpful working document to help them identify the best people and I have included a copy in the Appendices.

Perhaps more challenging is acknowledging that some clergy are in the wrong place. I know of a few clergy who are desperate to leave but have nothing to move on to. They are caught in an insecure place which becomes increasingly miserable. Mutually acceptable solutions have been found in many cases and these almost always start with honest conversations in safe environments. It is much better to have difficult conversations that move a challenging situation on than not having them and making that situation worse.

Supporting the well-being of resource church leaders is an important consideration, with such high expectations placed on them. Best practice here is when bishops intentionally pastor them with regular meetings and listen to the institutional challenges they are encountering. Sometimes they need help navigating them; other times we need to change the structures!

A challenge for diocesan staff working with resource churches is leadership continuity and staff alignment. There is a need to record what has been agreed and communicate decisions clearly and widely. Flexibility can be challenging but it is an important posture in missional situations. This has led to some exciting innovations, sometimes with early deployment of gifted ordinands and curates leading church plants, with proper supervision.

Lack of diocesan church-planting strategy

Dioceses need to invest time in developing a church-planting and revitalisation strategy so that the resource church can support its delivery. Without a plan, a diocese lurches from one missed opportunity to another. Setting a goal for planting is a good step forward but it's important to have a worked-through, consistent strategy to fully answer how that goal will be achieved. I suggest inviting resource church leaders to be part of the strategic conversation rather than excluding them. After all, they are a part of the solution to some of a diocese's challenges.

Setting a goal for planting is a good step forward but it's important to have a worked-through, consistent strategy

Lack of finances

Funding is linked with strategy. Alignment of resources is critical to making a vision and strategy happen in practice. That will inevitably mean that it is strategic what you do not fund as much as what you do. Church planting and revitalisation are part of a medium-term growth strategy and therefore directing funds towards this will produce a greater return in the future.

The complexity of buildings

Whether it is redeveloping older, listed church buildings, or buying and developing newer ones, buildings are a major issue for creating new resource churches. In particular, the amenity societies and the Diocesan Advisory Committee[175] can be extremely difficult to navigate. I believe we should try to simplify these structures to enable action. We can also learn from history. Extraordinary fundraising efforts, particularly in the 19th century, saw the building of hundreds of new churches in London and beyond.[176] On the other hand, perhaps it is time to give serious consideration to the church-planting movements in India, China and Africa, which created a low-cost structure precisely so that buildings are not a barrier to growth.[177]

Mission in difficult places

Planting churches is a challenge in tough inner-city areas, but the need is so great that it cannot be ignored. It is interesting to see the desire by many resource churches to plant onto housing estates and poorer areas. They continue to provide oversight and support while releasing and resourcing local leadership on the ground. The power relationships need to be attended to, but there is huge potential for grace to flow in both directions. Each of our plants in Tower Hamlets were into areas of extreme poverty, but it was such a blessing to us as a sending church to see and learn the ways that God worked in those contexts. Being in a network made a huge difference and meant we could do more together than we could alone. Some resource churches, like Woven[178] in Nottingham, are based around supporting multiple churches in deprived areas. Together, they are stronger and do much more than if they were separate parishes.

Being in a network made a huge difference and meant we could do more together than we could alone

Lack of will

If the bishop is keen but the diocesan team is not wholeheartedly behind a strategy for resource churches, it will never get the traction it needs to make a difference. I have heard some diocesan senior staff say, 'I'm not going to do it differently to how we've always done it.' Others have said, 'That's just not the way the Church of England works.' They seem to have no answer to the question posed by Lesslie Newbigin, 'Why their churches do not grow and why they are so little concerned about the multitudes who have not heard the gospel.'[179] Without this understanding, it will be very difficult to affect the change necessary to break through.

Change management

There are almost always barriers to any situation requiring change. They are not necessarily unreasonable, but if they are stopping the vision, then they need facing and acknowledging. In itself, this is the first stage in finding a way through them. Bishops need to be prepared to be leaders of disruptive change. They need teams who are with them in constructive and aligned ways. In any change situation, communication is vital at every stage, and no more so than with creating resource churches that plant and revitalise parish churches.

Bishops need to be prepared to be leaders of disruptive change

The challenges may be immense, but every time a plant happens there is a huge breakthrough, and it feels worth it enough to try again and again and again!

CHRIST CHURCH MAYFAIR

Diocese of London

> *Christ Church Mayfair in central London was planted from St Helen's Bishopsgate, London, in 2001. Led by **Matt Fuller**, it is committed to sharing the good news of Jesus Christ and has planted five churches, including sending a team to revitalise St Paul's Harringay, led by Pete Snow. Christ Church Mayfair was designated as a resource church in the Diocese of London in November 2018 by the Bishop of London, the Rt Revd and Rt Hon. Dame Sarah Mullally. Matt writes:*

The Lord Jesus himself said: 'It is more blessed to give than to receive..
ACTS 20:35

We shed tears over this Bible verse on 2 September 2018 as 32 adults and 12 children were sent from Christ Church Mayfair to Harringay in North London. We had to believe that it was more blessed to give away our dear friends than the church experience we knew and loved.

Christ Church Mayfair (CCM) had been planted in 2001 from St Helen's Bishopsgate with 90 people into a slightly derelict building in central London. The vision was always to be a church that would help to plant or revitalise other churches and, in God's kindness, we have been able to do that several times. We were designated a resource church in 2018 as a part of the Diocese of London's strategy to identify and support churches who have a vision to start new churches, revitalise existing parishes, and develop missionally minded leaders. Every parish in the diocese had an opportunity to express interest in becoming a resource church or to be revitalised, and it's hugely encouraging to be part of a diocesan-wide project to reach new people and grow our churches.

We built in leadership training from day one. It has broadly had three layers over the last 20 years. The first is our Discipleship Groups, which everyone is invited into as part of normal church life. The second is our Prepared to Serve course, which is a year out from Discipleship Groups for about 20 lay leaders to spend time with the vicar. They study Christian doctrine, Bible handling skills, and pastoral practice. The third layer is our Ministry Intern scheme, which has been training between three and eight interns every year for the past 20 years. Most of the plants/revitalisations we have been involved in have been led by someone who has been on the scheme, including Pete Snow. It gives those going real confidence.

We first began to consider trying to send a church plant to the Harringay area because we realised that we had a cohort of members who had settled in the same area. Maybe we should give them away to start or revitalise something?

We started praying about opportunities, getting out maps, and praying about the area. We wanted to come to help, not tread on anyone's toes, and so began conversations with the Bishops of Islington and Edmonton. Unknown to us, at the same time, the wardens of St Paul's Harringay were going into a vacancy, and asking their bishop for help in achieving the church's mission. So, the Bishop of Edmonton, the Rt Revd Rob Wickham, brokered some nervy first meetings between our potential planter, Pete Snow, and members of St Paul's PCC.

At CCM we developed different 'options' for how people could be involved. The 'gold' option was to join the launch team and uproot yourself from the resource church. The 'silver' option was being part of a 'SWAT' team: Servants Willing And Temporary. These were helpers who wanted to stay at CCM but who volunteered to be on a rota at St Paul's for the first year to help it get momentum. The 'bronze' level was to be a 'BOSS,' or Bums On Seats Sometimes. Just turn up occasionally and cheer us on!

Bishop Rob licensed Pete as a Curate in Charge in January 2018, and then we 'grafted' our Mayfair gang into St Paul's Harringay in September. The church doubled overnight, and the Junior Church restarted after several dormant years. Eighteen months later, we're by no means a big church, but the congregations have gone from 25 on a Sunday to 90, the income has tripled, and the church has gained crucial momentum. And for all this we thank God.

St Paul's was an Anglo-Catholic church by tradition, and CCM an evangelical one. That has meant we've needed to be careful and listen to what other people value. We have two services on a Sunday with different styles, but the same vicar and PCC. Our shared vision is to be 'a family on mission, treasuring Chris.'.

We deliberately built in the 'on mission' part to turn St Paul's outward. We threw open the doors of the building early on and started a 'pensioner and toddler' group on Tuesday mornings. This is now full, and we're about to start a seekers' course for those interested in Christianity. Young families are a prominent demographic in our neighbourhood, and when we spotted this early on we decided to resource the children's work wherever possible.

In addition, we decided to go door knocking every Sunday afternoon after church to meet people in the parish. One neighbour who has lived near St Paul's for 25 years gave me a good-natured telling-off the first time I met her: 'There are people in this neighbourhood who want to come to church. We've been waiting for you to knock on our door and invite us. What's taken you so long?!'

Another local sent me a lovely text message after his first visit to St Paul's in more than a decade: 'It was a renaissance. I literally wept to see the life that has been brought to my local church.' It's been moments like these that have helped me to see the resource church process in perspective: the city-centre resource church generously pumping resources out to the rest of the city, reaching locals in a way that was not happening before.

The Rt Revd Rob Wickham, Bishop of Edmonton

Overall, I welcome the concept of resource churches, and have four/five in my episcopal area. I am pleased that they speak into different ecclesiology; two being catholic and two/three being charismatic evangelical.

I valued enormously the process of designation, giving all churches the opportunity to self-designate as potential 'resource church' or 'church to be revitalised.' In reality, in this episcopal area, we have now revitalised St Philip the Apostle Tottenham, Christ Church Crouch End, St Paul's Haringey, St Peter le Poer Muswell Hill, and plans are becoming clearer to revitalise St Andrew's Alexandra Park, again in Muswell Hill. In addition, Faith House in Colindale was recently opened as a new church plant. Much of this has been enabled by resource churches, but not exclusively. Some plans for revitalisation have been explored and not been followed up (St Martin's Gospel Oak), where, in hindsight, God had a very impressive new parish priest for us to discern, and the church is now growing significantly. Other potential plants have been proven to be very difficult as a result of negotiating the threats and fear that exists, especially between parishes where resolutions or no resolutions are in place. We still have much trust to build. Despite these interventions, church attendance in Haringey continues to decline heavily (in 10 years from 1.4 per cent of the population attending to 0.9 per cent), but given most of these interventions are in Haringey, the prayer is that this decline will be stopped as a result.

St Paul's Harringay is a lovely example of listening to the people. For a significant number of years the church had been led by a dedicated group of priests and people, raised vocations, and loved the neighbourhood. The parish priest had been, for a while, the priest of a different parish, and curates have lived in the vicarage. When the parish priest and curate left fairly soon after each other, a quiet day was held by the PCC. In this quiet day, there was a real sense of God telling the lay people that they needed a fresh start; they wanted to develop ministry for themselves, and not be dependent upon a different parish for leadership, and they wanted their vicar to live in the parish. It then became obvious that their longer-term history had been of a different theological ecclesiology. A mapping exercise then took place, and it was discovered that several people living in the parish attended Christ Church Mayfair, so the curate, Pete Snow, was invited to meet with St Paul's to develop a potential church graft. This led to Pete being first licensed as Curate of the

Parish, and then as Vicar. This piece of intervention has led the church to grow significantly, and the local serving of the population in new ways has given the local church more prominence in the locality. It was also built upon the sacrificial giving of Christ Church (without which this would not have taken place) to a place of financial self-sufficiency, proving that such things are possible in areas of urban deprivation. Furthermore, building plans are now developing to help us serve the community further and proclaim the good news in Jesus Christ. I am delighted, as the bishop, to help enable this development in ministry to take place, especially as its inception came from the local congregation listening to God and reimagining their future. This was a fabulous example of bottom-up discernment and prophetic wisdom.

CHAPTER 10

EMERGING ALTERNATIVE MODELS OF RESOURCE CHURCHES

As different church traditions in the Church of England have begun to engage with the idea of resourcing the wider church for mission, other resource church models have emerged. The vast majority of resource churches have been set up along the lines of this book, but it is helpful and exciting to see how some resource churches are exploring different approaches to achieve a similar end – the growth and renewal of churches in dioceses. We need every tradition and every kind of church to reach everyone with the gospel.

We need every tradition and every kind of church to reach everyone with the gospel

Several of the cases in this chapter are from London Diocese due partly to the intentional push in 2018 to support churches of different traditions becoming resource churches. Altogether, 19 were appointed as such by Bishop Sarah Mullaly and I look at four here from different traditions, alongside two other different models of resource church elsewhere in the country.

St George-in-the-East

This modern Catholic resource church is based in Tower Hamlets, London, and led by Rector Richard Springer and supported by the Centre for Theology and Community (CTC) director Angus Ritchie. They use community organising practices to renew their tradition in this generation and they are already resourcing and working with churches in a wide variety of denominations and traditions.

They set up a Lay Community, rooted in prayer and trained in community organising, that led to congregational renewal at St George's and the planting of two new congregations, 'Choir Church,' a 40-strong monthly congregation in their parish school, and 'English, Prayer, Action,' a small but growing congregation of low-paid migrant workers. They are exploring two new church plants – one based around their 'Open Table on the Streets' homeless outreach and one aimed at isolated elderly people. Of the present and prospective church plants, all but Choir Church (which is led by a team of three, one of whom is ordained) are lay led. In time, they are planning to generate plants from each of these new congregations.

Through their partnership with CTC, they share their learning with other churches around East London and beyond, using learning communities focused on planting congregations in primary schools and making church accessible to those on the margins. They have curates who are planning to go on to lead renewal and planting in other churches when they finish their curacies. They feel particularly called to inner-city neighbourhoods and to those who are in some way marginalised within society, reflected in their focus to plant congregations among working-class communities, recent migrants and homeless people. See the case study on page 62 for the personal reflections of Angus Ritchie, Richard Springer and Bishop Joanne.

St Mary's Tottenham

This traditional Catholic resource church is located in North London and led by Fr Simon Morris. It is in an area of significant economic deprivation and ethnically 90 per cent BAME. Simon was first curate, then became vicar in 2011. They celebrated the reopening of The Good Shepherd Mission Church within the parish after 70 years of closure in 2012. St Mary's and the Good Shepherd have seen growth in recent years, especially among children and families. They were excited about becoming a resource church in order to support the revitalisation of St Philip's South Tottenham, two parishes and a mile away, and try to work out how that might be possible in a traditional Catholic setting.

In 2018, Fr Lee Clark was appointed to St Philip's as priest-in-charge and initially worked alongside Fr Simon to try to take a planting team with him to St Philip's. The intention was for St Mary's to send some people to help the other church and support them as much as possible, especially by sending people to support their Sunday Masses. Sadly, the team did not materialise, and Fr Lee went alone to St Philip's. Over the last three years, the church has grown from a very low base to a regular 50 with more baptisms in 2019 pre-Covid than there had been in the last 30 years. They had 300 at their carol service, most of whom had never been to church before.

Both Frs Simon and Lee are extraordinary leaders bringing congregational renewal and missional energy. The revitalisation of St Philip's cannot really be linked to St Mary's other than by prayer and encouragement and this might say something of the close-knit and local community that is based at St Mary's and their relative lack of mobility.

Preston Minster

Philip North, Bishop of Burnley, was determined to enable traditional Catholics to learn how to plant churches again since it was so much part of their history in the 19th century. He worked in partnership with Holy Trinity Brompton (HTB) to invite them to plant a resource church in Preston Minster in 2019 which would be intentionally linked to neighbouring St George's, which has an Anglo-Catholic tradition. This became the Preston Resourcing Parish, where Fr David Craven, based at St George's, joined the staff team of the overall leader, Sam Haigh. They received £1.5M from Strategic Development Funding based across Preston Minster and St George's to help them to resource churches across the city and county. The focus initially went on building the congregations up to reach out to the unchurched of the city, including the significant local student population, with a combination of an outward-looking focus, sacrificial generosity, excellence, boldness, hospitality and creativity, and this is all part of the Diocesan Vision 2026.

It was the first resourcing church partnership with HTB in Lancashire, and the first in the country to partner with a traditional Anglo-Catholic parish. Preston Minster is now preparing to plant a new resource church in Blackburn and one in Blackpool. St George's is preparing to launch an Anglo-Catholic tradition plant in the near future. The minster is closely supported by HTB's planting charity CRT, who are training the resource church planters.

There is much riding on this as it attempts to break down many of the barriers between traditions. Much will depend on the relationship between the two church leaders at the heart of the resourcing parish and how flexible they are to apply the learning into practice. See page 77 for the personal reflections of Sam Haigh and Bishop Philip.

St Martin-in-the-Fields

Located in Trafalgar Square, London, St Martin's is the home of the recently formed HeartEdge network that is about equipping the 'broad middle' of the church to increase numbers of committed disciples and to grow congregations. Its vision is: 'At the Heart. On the Edge: Appealing to the heart, in the heart of London, and ministering to the edges of society, at the cutting edge of innovation in culture, commerce, charity and congregational lif'. In recent years it has created new congregations alongside the Sunday services, including Bread for the World, International Group with asylum seekers and Great Sacred Music. Since 2017, HeartEdge has already become an ecumenical network drawn to a mission model of compassion, commerce, culture and congregation.

St Martin's offers HeartEdge to resource and renew churches in the diocese, aiming to engage 30 churches over three years – structured into three hubs of 10 churches – to help them to grow healthy, sustainable and dynamic kingdom communities. They believe growth in numbers of disciples arises out of congregations discovering new ways of being church. To support this, they share existing mission projects – like Disability Advisory Groups, Great Sacred Music, Inspired to Follow Enquirers' course, International Groups, Stand-up Theology, Start:Stop and the Nazareth Community – with these churches. Their hope is that this combination, which includes all kinds of people, will enable churches of all traditions to find their own way to becoming abundant communities. Through this approach, St Martin's would love to galvanise the broad church 'from disempowered retrospection to joyful missio'.

Their hope is that this combination, which includes all kinds of people, will enable churches of all traditions to find their own way to becoming abundant communities

This is not intentionally a church planting resource model but rather the offer of a complementary strand of mission through partnership. I think the difference is summed up well in Sam Well's phrase, that 'you can do unbelievable things together if you start with one another's assets rather than deficit'. It will be interesting to follow their journey as a resource church, and particularly as they resource other churches to encourage their growth.

Woven, Nottingham

Woven is a family of seven churches in Nottingham. This 'church of churches' is part of a city-wide strategy for growing churches led by Bishop Paul Williams. St Margaret's Aspley is the larger resource church, forming the 'hub' to support ministry and mission across five existing parishes in North Nottingham ministering to deprived outer-urban estates in Bilborough, Broxtowe, Cinderhill and Basford. Each of the seven churches has its own flavour and is focused on its own locality. They have a common vision – to call Nottingham to the wonder and way of Jesus – and have shared resources, shared leadership and a unified mission, hence the name 'Woven.'

The combined population of the five parishes is over 60,000 people with current church attendance at 0.7 per cent of those. Rich Atkinson leads the new team at St Margaret's, Aspley with an operations manager, and worship and youth minister. While their main focus is towards growing new disciples there, they also have responsibilities and oversight for the wider network of churches.

As the 'hub' church, St Margaret's is instrumental in helping initiate and support new worshipping communities in Bilborough, Broxtowe and Basford, with new services complementing existing small and elderly congregations. Rich leads a team of four associate missioners who are leading new worshipping communities on the estates. Each one brings distinctive gifts and experience to the wider team, covering children and families work, performing arts and youth work, worship and community engagement, and they are part of a well-defined 'gospel partnership' led by Rich at St Margaret's.

Rather than waiting for the resource church to be built up first, this model sees the group of churches being revitalised together, saving costs and spreading expertise and gifting across all the churches. The biggest challenge for them is to do ministry on a large scale in a place with high urban deprivation, but there is a huge benefit in the ability to share resources across a group of churches rather than going it alone. Church planting for Woven will be about planting new congregations to reach different communities in specific localities or particular people groups. See Bishop Paul's reflections on page 126 for more on Woven.

Rather than waiting for the resource church to be built up first, this model sees the group of churches being revitalised together, saving costs and spreading expertise and gifting across all the churches

One Church Harrow

Three churches in Harrow, West London, have come together for a single purpose: to see 10 per cent of the borough of Harrow following Jesus in 10 years. They believe the most effective way to do this is through multiple church planting. To that end, they are working together on evangelism, disciple-making and leadership development. They do not see themselves as the one church of Harrow, but they do want to see the churches of Harrow acting together as one, to all play a part in a new church planting movement across the borough. Since 2020, they have planted Mosaic, an intercultural church plant led by a bi-vocational ordained leader, Mohan Seevaratnam, and they are planting another church in Harrow called Hope Church. They have plans for many more.

They seek to reflect their community and to catalyse a church planting movement using many different expressions of church in schools, community centres, coffee shops and homes

They describe themselves as families on mission seeing many churches planted, led by lay and ordained ministers, helping and equipping Christians to be effective disciples in their everyday lives. Their strategy includes a regular united rhythm of prayer, Alpha invitations, loving and sharing faith with neighbours, growth through midweek 'Circle' groups for intentional discipleship, training and developing leaders from different ethnic, cultural and socio-economic backgrounds. In everything, they seek to reflect their community and to catalyse a church planting movement using many different expressions of church in schools, community centres, coffee shops and homes.

It is a bold vision, drawing on thinking from around the world and learning from church planting in different parts of London and the rest of the country. They have intentionally lowered the bar on church leadership, not in quality but in accessibility, by positioning their training so that every leader in the church recognises their own potential as a future church planter. Their challenge will be to develop these leaders and support them, with energy and vision, within an Anglican framework without it hemming them in. As they have seen elsewhere, such as in Southall's missionally focused churches, mission is massively enhanced when churches trust each other and work together.

Are they resource churches?

Can the churches above be described accurately as resource churches as I have defined them? Using the five-fold definition in Chapter 1, these churches have all been designated by their bishops and are joining in with a diocesan strategy to evangelise a city or town and transform society. They are intentionally resourced with curates to revitalise the church and they provide resources for mission across their town or city. Where they may differ is how overt they are about planting, or revitalising parishes through planting, and in building a leadership pipeline to enable this. The standout exception is St Martin-in-the-Fields and this was explicitly part of our arrangement when they were appointed. Their focus is on resourcing churches with vision, ministries and support to develop a similar missional approach to compassion, commerce, culture and congregation engagement and development. They might go on to revitalise a parish church but that is not part of their vision for now.

It is so exciting to see these churches wrestling with the challenge of renewal and growth in the Church of England and seeing them engage with the national movement of resource churches being designated around the country by their local bishops. I spend much of my time nationally and in London Diocese working with cohorts of resource church leaders and their teams, encouraging them to learn from one another. It takes time to build the trust for this to happen. In London we have gathered the 19 church cohort three times a year in a learning community, with regular updates and input to draw out maximum shared learning and application. Over time, there have been growing levels of trust, mutual learning and encouragement, heightened by a real buzz of being on mission together.

Each of these churches has chosen their own pathway to revitalisation and growth and there is much to learn as each one develops. All are passionate about seeing the wider Church renewed and they all want to play their part. The biggest challenge for any of these alternative models will be to choose to work together rather than going it alone. This is the danger of any tradition in the Church of England, but its strength comes from welcoming every part rather than demonising difference. Institutions like the Church of England have a tendency to water down ambitious movements to minimise change to itself. If we can keep encouraging these resource churches to revitalise parishes and continue to plant new churches, with all the strengths and emphases that different traditions bring, then something extraordinary could happen across the Church. May it be so!

All are passionate about seeing the wider Church renewed and they all want to play their part

TELFORD MINSTER

Diocese of Lichfield

Telford is the largest town in Shropshire and one of the fastest growing towns in the UK. With a younger than average population, Telford Minster overlaps Lichfield and Hereford Dioceses. Telford Minster began officially in 2020 as a resource church, operating under a Bishop's Mission Order (BMO) granted by the Bishop of Lichfield. It will be based in the town centre, with community groups spread across the town and surrounding housing estates. It is led by **Revd Matt Beer**, *who writes:*

Telford has a population of 180,000 people, but fewer than 1,000 people across all denominations currently meet as 'the Church.' Our aim is to plant a resource church to reach some of the other 179,000 people over the next six years, as we dream huge dreams and pray earnestly for the people of Telford to encounter Jesus. We plan to gather in a central location, between the shopping centre and cinema, and surrounded by cafés and restaurants, serving as a minster to resource mission across the town.

Because we are looking to reach those who currently have no or little faith, we are continuing to dream about what the Church should really look like in Telford. We are excited to see what the Lord is going to be doing, and we particularly aim to reach the under 40s.

Just three of us began the planting team from our home in October 2019, and by April 2020 this had grown to a team of 26, with around 45 people engaging with us in person for Alpha, services, or other gatherings. We have developed a vision team who are praying hard for what the Lord is doing here. Over the first six months, we settled into Telford well and began to make in-roads into our community through schools' work, occasional offices, being visible and approachable, and attending key events in the community. We also visited and started building relationships with every church in Telford and the entire area of the BMO.

We are passionate about not overwhelming other churches nearby, but are working with them and alongside them so that all the churches of Telford can grow. The support we have had from our area bishop Sarah Bullock, as well as our diocesan CEO/Secretary Julie Jones has been invaluable, and we've been encouraged to see many other leaders embrace what we are doing and hear their prayers for us.

During the Covid-19 pandemic, the team was adaptable, and despite a delay in the building schedule and other additional challenges, we had some amazing opportunities and saw God at work through these. We soon grew out of our home base, so when gathering had to stop because of the pandemic we were able to move online. The fact that we didn't yet have a building of our own allowed us to transition to online naturally and also model a different sort of church. We've continued to build community online, with people finding out about us through social media and word of mouth. Over a 'Sabbath rest' in the summer of 2020, we ran some socially distanced informal gatherings including picnics, prayer walks, and a cream tea.

We have spent time building a strong team that was hard at work though the ups and downs of lockdown. We licensed our associate minister during this time, and recruited several positions: our operations manager, whose big task is to oversee the building and give us an outward perspective on church operations; our youth pastor, who is passionate about detached youth work and the marginalised; our children and schools pastor, who is already at work in 15 schools in Telford; and our worship and media pastor, whose skills and passion have enabled us to engage with many people who would never have set foot through the doors of a church building.

As a resource church we want to share what we have with others in nearby churches and more widely, so we keep in touch with what is going on locally, finding ways we can support and resource others rather than doubling up on what other churches are doing. We do, though, want to seize opportunities where there are projects, which as a resource church we are well placed to engage with so everyone can benefit. For example, we are partnering with The Children's Society to film a short Christingle video which we hope will be used by teachers and group leaders in Telford and beyond.

We are still working out exactly what our church will look like, but part of our vision is to plant between six and 10 minster communities across the town. We were encouraged to launch the first of these into a local estate. At first we had to work within pandemic restrictions and the 'rule of six' that applied at the time, so our communities were limited in number, but actually this was a great model. Two leaders chose four others to begin each community, and we have another four leaders ready to launch another two communities when we can. These will be on both new-build and existing housing estates, enabling uniquely contextual mission, especially in places that some in Telford have said the Church has forgotten. All these leaders are under 30 as we feel that God is calling us particularly to the high percentage of younger age groups in Telford.

Our first year was not without its challenges, not only because of Covid-19 but also due to the very nature of arriving in a new place and starting something from scratch. Telford is a new town with very little tradition, so building relationships has been quite difficult, however we're working on these and feel encouraged with the progress we're making.

Alongside the challenges there have been some exciting things to encourage us, including:

- Four people have come to faith in Jesus Christ with baptisms to follow.

- Our first week out of lockdown we baptised someone who came to a service after a prophetic word was given.

- The rapid growth of people coming along who are not rooted in local churches.

- The wider community reaction when told what we planned to do.

- The local schools' enthusiasm for a new church reaching younger demographics.

As we look ahead, we anticipate the completion of our building and, with our team now in place and increasing capacity, we are excited to see more impact in the town. Telford Miister has already proven to be worth the investment, prayer, fasting, and envisioning, as we are already seeing some of the fruit. It's proving to be a fulfilment of the yearning of the hearts of God and his people.

The Rt Revd Dr Michael Ipgrave, Bishop of Lichfield

The decision to establish a new church in the new town of Telford came from a realisation that our Christian mission across the town was in urgent need of rejuvenation. Telford is a predominantly young town, with 70 per cent of the population under 50 years of age and 25 per cent under 18; this is a demographic very different from that of our established parish congregations. Moreover, our churches are located in the historic village, small town, and industrial settlements which predated the creation of the new town five decades ago; we had no worshipping and missional presence in the modern town centre, the shopping and recreational hub which now attracts people from across Telford and beyond. Recognising that, within the diocese as a whole, Telford had for years felt rather marginalised; we felt that a new church here would make a powerful statement of commitment to several communities which might feel peripheral.

One of the priorities in laying the groundwork of the new Telford Miister has been to work hard at the relational matrix of other churches, both Church of England parishes and ecumenical partner churches, within which this new centre of worship and mission finds its place. Both in the formation of the successful bid to the church commissioners' Strategic Development Funding and in the first months of the minster team's pioneering work, considerable energy was expended in meeting with, listening to, and reassuring ministerial colleagues that the minster was offered as an additional resource rather than presented as a competitive threat. Inevitably, there were anxieties and concerns to be attended to, and it has also been important for this new Christian presence both to honour the long-standing witness of older churches and to learn from their wisdom. Care has also been taken over details such as the timing of worship and the communication of information. As a result, it has been possible to show in practice that the minster is not interested in receiving already committed Christian disciples from other churches, but is seeking to reach out to those without a current active Christian faith commitment, whether they are de-churched or unchurched.

The numerical growth of the new congregation, from less than five to almost 50 in the space of nine months, has been both sustained and impressive, all the more so given that the greater part of the initial months was during the period of Covid-related lockdown, with first closure of and then restrictions on places of worship. Zoom has been a shaping medium in the formation of the new minster's life, and this has led to an emphasis on face-to-face participation in worship, the deepening of interpersonal relationships, and a strong sense of defined and repeated commitment – rather than logging into a pre-recorded broadcast, people have to receive and respond to a personal invitation. When the minster congregation was able to meet again in person, the temporary location chosen to meet (pending the availability of the intended town centre venue) was one of the old parish churches. Intriguingly, the morning parish congregation here has grown concurrently with the afternoon minster gathering – a real sign of God multiplying blessings in an unexpected way, and perhaps a pointer to the way in which our hope and prayer is that Telford Minster will become a blessing to all the Christian churches of Telford and to the wider diocese.

CHAPTER 11

THE FUTURE OF RESOURCE CHURCHES

What part will resource churches have to play in the future of the Church of England? Since this book is being written after a year of global pandemic it is hard to predict anything with precise accuracy. There are signs of hope alongside signs of discouragement. Even before Covid-19, the institutional Church was in decades of decline and yet there is a movement of churches that are growing and planting and welcoming new people who are coming to faith in Jesus. Where do resource churches fit in all of this?

At the beginning of the 2020s, the Church of England began to engage in a vision, led by Archbishop Stephen Cottrell, to be Christ-centred and Jesus-shaped, becoming simpler, humbler and bolder. It is to be a church of missionary disciples, where mixed ecology is the norm, and must be younger and more diverse. A 'mixed ecology' can be characterised by a proliferation of mission initiatives, church plants, fresh expressions, new religious communities, and online communities of faith. If every parish becomes involved, there could be over 10,000 new churches[180] of various kinds, where new people are reached in new places in new ways.

The creation of new churches through church planting and parish revitalisation are at the heart of this vision. They are not the only way this mixed ecology will grow but when new churches are planted or brought back to life, there is a missionary zeal and energy that sparks new life and new initiatives, stirring new ways of evangelism and mission. Resource churches will be at the vanguard of this work and we are seeing the first fruits of what God is doing through them as they plant and revitalise parishes around their towns, cities and dioceses.

Resource churches will be at the vanguard of this work

When I first started putting numerical goals on what we thought would meet this vision, I guessed that we needed perhaps 200 resource churches in England's 60 largest cities and towns. If they could be enabled to plant and revitalise churches in those urban areas, then there was a good chance that that would catalyse a change in the church attendance figures which were consistently lower there than in other places. If 100 resource churches were appointed by 2025, then 200 might be possible by 2030. In fact, by the end of 2020, 100 resource churches had been created and designated by their bishops, five years ahead of our faith schedule. Imagine what might happen if they all went on to plant multiple churches!

I have seen first-hand the impact of resource churches, from my experience at Holy Trinity Brompton (HTB) and when we did our own church planting in the East End of London. I have had the privilege of supporting the growing movement of resource churches from different networks, and increasingly different traditions, which are doing extraordinary work in challenging places all around the country. They are changing England's cities and towns.

These churches, that lean naturally towards mission and those outside the Church, have responded in incredible ways during the Covid-19 pandemic, gearing quickly to ministry online, working out how to increase their evangelistic reach, and responding with practical love in communities at a scale that has left some councils and community organisations speechless. Where some churches battened down the hatches to weather the storm, these churches have grown. Their church planting and revitalisations have gone on in spite of the challenges, in some cases slower, in others at pace. The opportunities for revitalisations are only going to increase as some pre-Covid decline has accelerated through the tragic impact of a year of lockdowns. They are not the only churches that have learned how to adjust to these circumstances quickly, but they have been at the frontline of innovation and missional engagement. It is interesting to see how many resource churches used their ambition, scale and ability to adapt quickly to the pandemic in particular ways.

Being creative with evangelism

When the first lockdown happened in England in March 2020, church buildings were closed, and there was a scramble to learn new skills and procure new equipment to stream online. Many resource churches already had technical facilities and the necessary expertise to switch services and church ministries, including the Alpha course, online. HTB, who pioneered Alpha, soon realised that new online groups could be started every week, rather than waiting for the next course to begin two or three months later. When the first lockdown was relaxed, these churches began to welcome people who had attended online Alpha, come to faith in Jesus and were now hungry to meet Christians in person for the first time. Resource churches worked hard in innovative ways on these connections and saw their churches growing with new local contacts as a result.

Responding with compassion

Like several other resource churches, Hackney Church operated a food bank and kitchen that already provided 5,000 meals before lockdown. In 2020, they served 250,000 meals to poor and struggling families in Hackney and in each of the other four locations that they had been invited to revitalise. During the lockdown, one of their new locations was St Leonard's Shoreditch, locally led by ordinands, under the oversight of Hackney Church leader Al Gordon.

Harbour Church Portsmouth set up an online link to enable people to access food parcels and care packages aimed at teenagers, students and families who may have been too embarrassed to come in person. Parcels were then delivered to the door within 24 hours, together with details of other help available from the church and other local agencies.

St Mary's Andover worked with the local NHS and GP surgeries to support people isolated in the community. They created the 'Phone Friends' project, connecting patients with members of the community for a weekly call to talk 'about anything and everything,' connecting isolated people with the outside world. Likewise, Gas Street Birmingham set up a befriending project, making over 450 befriending calls in a few months to lonely and isolated people in the community.

And on a national scale, HTB set up the Love Your Neighbour campaign in which their network of churches raised funding and donations to provide 4 million meals for poor and marginalised people and made 15,000 calls to people in isolation.

Still planting but adapting

In June 2020, during the middle of the pandemic, Alex and Laura Rayment moved to Liverpool to create a resource church by revitalising St Barnabas Penny Lane, where Paul McCartney had sung in the choir as a boy. It was hard for the Rayments, without much face-to-face contact, to envision and encourage the 25-strong team who had moved to Liverpool from around the country. They began to build community from scratch, on walks with just one or two others. Alex said, 'Even in the midst of a global pandemic, God built his church. God was definitely not in lockdown!' They grew many relationships from cold contacts, through Instagram and their website, and they started to see local people join the church in greater numbers – through quiz nights, online services and engaging with families and young people. Certainly though, it was a challenge. Alex's motto was, 'Plan for a week, prepare for a fortnight and dream for a month,' such was the need for flexibility. They had over 30 on their first online Alpha course and started a new worship service online, even before their church building was ready, and people were committing to join the church before they had even come in person. One of the ways they adapted was through a focus on social transformation ministry. Alex described it as their new operating system rather than just a sideline. Partly due to the pandemic, the vision for the church was realigned to those on the edges coming to the centre, with love being experienced by the marginalised, hurting, those in poverty and those physically distanced.

Other new resource churches were also planted in the middle of Covid-19, like Nelson Street Church in the Manchester Diocese. Janie and James Cronin launched online *Other new resource* *churches were also* *planted in the middle* *of Covid-19* in March 2021 with a particular emphasis on reaching under 40s, especially youth and children, and they spent lockdown prayer walking the streets, building a team, connecting and praying with leaders of other local churches.

Diocesan decisions were being made during the pandemic too. In his address to the diocesan synod in November 2020, Paul Butler, Bishop of Durham, announced, 'We have been further supported to develop seven resource churches that will in due course plant out to revitalise or develop new congregations, including a brand-new congregation starting from scratch in Wynyard, Stockton-on-Tee'. Rather than reducing their ambition after such a challenging time, Durham Diocese chose to build on and increase the impact that resource churches would make on their plans going forwards.

Joining in with the national vision

It was encouraging to see resource churches tackling the challenges of the pandemic in so many different ways. Looking forward, they have a critical part to play in the national Church's vision. Many hundreds of parish churches will be revitalised, bringing new life to their local contexts and fresh energy for the wider Church. In addition, they will have catalysed the planting and revitalising of many other churches alongside them. Over the coming years, we will watch and pray with interest to see how they develop and play their part in God's plans for his Church in this country.

TOP CHURCH

Diocese of Worcester

*In 2017 the future of Top Church looked uncertain due to a declining congregation and at-risk building. However, the Bishops of Worcester and Dudley decided to seize this opportunity by creating a new resource church led by **James and Esther Treasure** in 2018. It's grown to around 150 people and has plans to plant another church in 2022. Its heart is to serve the most vulnerable in the community, helping the people in Dudley and beyond to experience 'life in all its fullness' as Jesus promised. James says:*

I was a minister in an independent evangelical church for about 20 years in the borough of Dudley, but I began to feel that God was calling me to be ordained in the Church of England. The suffragan Bishop of Dudley at the time, Bishop Graham Usher, who is now the Bishop of Norwich, was hugely supportive and made this possible. During this period, the Diocese of Worcester was hoping to start a resource church and Dudley, in the northern part of the diocese, was a potential location. Dudley is the poorest parish in our diocese – it's very urban with high unemployment and low life expectancy. There were seven Anglican churches in the town but none of the congregations were over 20 people, and there wasn't much vision or mission for Dudley. So the Diocese of Worcester thought a resource church would bring a new sense of energy and life to the area. After I got ordained, Bishop Graham approached me with the suggestion of leading this new church due to my background in an evangelical, charismatic church and my local connections in the area. I was reluctant at first – I was hoping we might return to London! But I thought, 'I've got to do thi.'.

Dudley hasn't got a university or a big young adult population, and all the schools are failing apart from one, so it's a really impoverished area. The context is different from typical resource churches in cities which often thrive on university students and young adults with lots of energy and aspirations. It's a challenging situation and as a historically non-conformist and Methodist area, the Anglican Church has never truly thrived here. The vision, supported by the Bishops of Worcester and Dudley, and the Archdeacon of Dudley, Nikki Groarke, was to create a thriving Anglican church that was mission-focused. And so, at Top Church (officially named St Thomas and St Luke's) we began laying foundations for this in October 2018.

We didn't come with a team or have much money when we started so we began from quite a low base level, but there were about 60 people who were interested when we put out a call to come and help us plant. We are quite Anglican: we have liturgy and I wear a dog collar, and we chose not to partner with Holy Trinity Brompton or New Wine as we felt the model and approach of each of these would not fit easily within Dudley. I also believe church planting should be highly contextual and my concern was that a strongly branded approach could overpower this. One of our aims is to be a real blessing to our community as there is a deep level of need in Dudley, so social action is high on our agenda. For example, when we put our Strategic Development Funding bid together for the Church of England, I asked for the role of a worship leader to be replaced by a community worker, as we needed that more in Dudley. We actually got both in the end, but I wanted to prioritise the needs of the community and steer us in this direction as a church. Our heart is to get out into the community, working with people and sharing God's love. In some ways, we are trying to function more like a traditional parish, transforming the place as well as the people.

Kath is our community minister and the first part of her job was to research the area to find out what the needs were and what was being done to meet those needs. We didn't want to reinvent the wheel. After mapping all these different areas, we then launched a couple of community activities. We're part of the growing network 'Places of Welcome,' where we open up the church and create a community hub. It's for people who are addicts, in debt, homeless, or refugees. We welcome them, give them a cup of tea and a sense of belonging, and then signpost them to places that can help. Toddler Town is another project that we've started, which is particularly for isolated mums and dads. Another area we are developing is chaplaincy. The church has become chaplain to a housing association that runs a refuge for domestic abuse victims in the town and also houses vulnerable people. All our staff are involved in this. We're also chaplain to a big further education college, which has never had any Christian presence before, and all the senior schools in the area. We've become our own charitable trust so we can work across the borough of Dudley.

One of my favourite stories is about a lady called Sam and her husband. Sam had always wanted to come to church but was worried that she wouldn't be welcomed. But one day she turned up and loved it, and after having a meaningful encounter with God, she decided that she wanted to be baptised alongside her daughter. On her baptism day, Sam brought all her family along, including her mum who had been going through an ancestry website. Her mum had recently discovered that Sam's great-great-great-great-grandparents were married in Top Church on the exact same date (21 April) that Sam was being baptised on, nearly two centuries before in 1834. Everyone had goosebumps hearing this – it definitely felt more than a coincidence. The church has been here for hundreds of years and it feels like this place is rediscovering its ministry and identity.

Another great story about someone finding a home is a lad called Josh, who we baptised a few months ago. Josh had never really felt accepted in any church but he came along and found a home here. He brought his whole family along to his baptism and confessed his faith in Christ in front of everyone. We love that people are finding a community here, especially those who never felt like they belonged anywhere. We're finding that growth is happening slowly – rather than huge numbers coming to Christ at one service, we're journeying with individual people and they are gradually finding faith. Often the people we are meeting need a lot of personal care so it's great to see individual lives being changed. We get a lot of visitors too, which is great, so we're reaching new people. Our worshipping community is now around 150 and we hope to plant again in two years' time.

One of our phrases is that we want to 'build a bigger table' – we want to have a big table for communion where everyone is welcome. Christ promises his presence in the bread during communion, so we aim to make this a priority. Some churches have big bands for their worship or big stages for their preachers, but our hope is to have a bigger table where all are welcomed in the name of Jesus. We are, in fact, building such a table at the moment using wood from our old pews! This excites us and there's so much prophetic imagery in this too. So, we have communion regularly and eat together after our services. Our worship style is mixed – we'll have charismatic worship songs but the shape of the service is more Anglican as we have communion and time in the Word. We used to say that we were evangelical in the pulpit (preaching Jesus from the Scriptures for conversion), charismatic in our worship, and sacramental around the altar (we believe something happens in the bread and wine). It's also great to have people from different traditions in our congregation and see them appreciating the different parts of our services. Some people, who have been very rooted in the Anglican tradition, initially might feel at home in the communion but struggle with some of the charismatic worship, but over time, we see them really engaging with the worship. Others might at first disengage with the liturgy, but slowly start to understand the power and beauty of the words during communion.

There have definitely been challenges because of the area that we live in – we're opposite local drug dealers, and the first time we opened our doors, my wife's purse got stolen. Also, the church building has taken up a lot of time as it was placed on the 'at risk' register and needed major repair work. But we are passionate about creating a thriving Anglican church for Dudley and we feel that the renewal of the Church will come from the poor places. We can put a lot of pressure on ourselves when we compare ourselves to other resource churches, but we love seeing what God is doing and being part of this town's story.

The Rt Revd Dr John Inge, Bishop of Worcester

The vision of a resourcing church (our preferred term in this diocese) in Dudley goes back at least 10 years. When I learned of the HTB plant at St Peter's Brighton, I wrote to Nicky Gumbel to ask, 'What about Dudley?' At that stage, understandably, he had more than enough with which to cope. The impetus to turn vision into reality came some years later with support from the national Church in the form of Strategic Development Funding.

Having initially begun negotiations with HTB and Gas Street Birmingham, it was providential that the wonderful James Treasure, previously leader of a non-denominational church in the metropolitan borough of Dudley, was coming to the end of a brief curacy. He had been ordained after finding a vocation to minister in the Church of England and now felt called to lead our resourcing church in Dudley, something which we felt was providential. I had no major misgivings other than a worry over whether the new church would be welcomed by our other churches. The fact that James is known and trusted by them has made a huge difference.

James has been and remains a major source of encouragement to us. The biggest challenge has been the building. We were convinced that it was right to locate the resourcing church in St Thomas and St Luke's – 'Top Church' – in Dudley, the civic church of the borough and an iconic building in the community. Our determination that the new congregation could be located there rather than in a warehouse, for example, was based on our knowledge of the area, though it was not a strategy with which HTB, in our early conversations, were happy. Fortunately, we have been successful in a large National Lottery Heritage Fund bid to finance major necessary repairs, though managing that at the same time as launching the new church has been a major strain on James.

The church attracted a regular congregation of 100 or so before it had even been launched and the initial signs are very encouraging indeed. It is growing at a fast rate. The real test, of course, will come when Top Church is able to plant and resource other churches in the area. We have begun conversations about this and I am very hopeful that this will go well.

My view of resourcing churches has not changed greatly as a result of this experience, though I am more than ever convinced both of their value and of the necessity of working with the Spirit so as to adapt the vision for individual circumstances. This particular example has not turned out as I would have predicted: it's much more exciting. Such is God's providence.

Resourcing churches are a vital – though not exclusive – plank in our commitment to reach people with the good news of Jesus Christ. I am more than ever convinced of the important part that resourcing churches can play, alongside parish churches, in the renewal and growth of the Church and the spread of the gospel.

CONCLUSION

Looking back on those dreams under a blue sky in Portugal, we have come a long way. We dreamt of churches multiplying across the country, beginning in cities and planting and revitalising churches all across their regions that would reverse decline and ignite the Church into growth. The rough map we drew sketching out four church-planting churches on a flipchart have become 100 resource churches, living and breathing, growing and impacting their local communities, regions and dioceses. And even though it is not a new idea, the Church of England has embraced these church-planting churches into their strategies and structures so that the growth they have experienced might complement all the other areas for growth we long to see.

The rough map we drew sketching out four church-planting churches on a flipchart have become 100 resource churches

Since those daring dreams, I have had the great privilege of seeing many of our resource churches grow from the earliest stages of conception to their launch and even on to celebrate new plants from the churches they first planted. The processes behind these stages can be long and painful at times, yet also hugely rewarding and joyful. Just like giving birth to a child and seeing them grow to maturity and then go on to have their own children. And just like life, there are challenges.

I was struck by two conversations that I had today. One was with a cohort of resource church leaders, each of whom had planted a network of churches. The other was with my friend, and former Shadwell colleague, Rich Grant, who planted into St George's Gateshead, a resource church in Durham Diocese. These two contexts are very different but each one is challenging. Planting networks of churches requires bishops and archdeacons to re-engineer pastoral schemes when current structures cannot cope with the growth that is going on. Revitalising a church in Gateshead, doing mission in some of the most deprived wards in the country and preparing to plant further churches in the city, is an incredibly difficult context. The leaders I spoke to are outstanding in so many ways, leading churches that are making an extraordinary impact on their communities and bucking trends in the wider Church.

There are so many signs of hope coming from resource churches up and down the country. But in our ecclesiastical landscape, they are still relatively new, and they will continue to face many challenges because they are changing the status quo of the Church. Let me outline some of these challenges as I conclude.

Challenges for bishops and dioceses

The relationship between the bishop and resource church leader will be a vital one to nurture and it will remain critical in the years to come. The nature of this relationship in ecclesiastical terms is still being worked out. Resource churches are the new minster churches, different to local parish churches, and therefore they should be treated differently. These leaders will push boundaries – in good ways I hope – and I would expect there to be friction as new perspectives and approaches are tried out. But the rewards of staying well-connected will be worth it because of what can be achieved by this kind of missional partnership.

As we have seen, it is vital for bishops and senior diocesan teams to ensure that resource churches are connected into their diocesan strategies. There is a delicate balance here – not to favour the resource church over others, but to recognise their unique role and therefore to invite them into strategic conversations and planning. They are only part of what a diocese will be encouraging missionally, but they can play a role in catalysing other church planting, pioneering and fresh expression development. As a focus for unity, bishops can help to join all of this together.

Challenges for resource church leaders

The posture to lead a resource church requires ambitious faith and a humble heart, a generosity of spirit and an active pursuing of the unity of the Church. This is an active choice, even in the face of criticism and defensiveness. So much is required of any church leader, but resource church leaders have an even greater opportunity to influence if they choose. They can play their part in a bigger vision, including speaking into the bishop's wider strategy with humility and respect. They can offer resources and prayer and encouragement with huge generosity to the wider church with a desire to complement other mission that is going on rather than solely ploughing their own furrow. They can pray, not just for their own mission and ministry, but they can invite other churches to pray with them for the renewal of the whole Church and the transformation of society. This posture calls for wisdom, perseverance, patience and love. The rewards will catalyse a multiplying mission beyond anything we could dream of doing on our own.

Challenges for the Church of England

We must focus on those who do not come to church, rather than looking at the differences we have among ourselves. By focusing our mission on those outside the Church, we celebrate our diversity because our approach can be broader and connects more widely. The opposite makes us inward-looking and unattractive. Church planting, and the resource churches that are called upon to do this costly work again and again, does not need to be a threat. We need new churches to reach new people in new places in new ways and we need our struggling churches to be revitalised. We need a both-and approach rather than an either-or one. We need every size of church from every tradition and every missional movement to play their part, praying and praying for Jesus to build his church and for God's kingdom to come.

A critical factor in the years to come will be whether the Church of England can adapt its structures to be more agile with its processes. Some things need to take time to properly work through and process, but other matters do seem to be needlessly bound by red tape and bureaucracy. I do so appreciate the work my colleague and friend, Bishop Pete Broadbent has done nationally with simplification, and this work should also cover the pioneers and planters at the edge of the Church. We will need processes and models where we can start new churches quickly and robustly.

If we can meet these challenges, and inhabit these postures of faith and humility, generosity and unity, we will start to see these resource churches playing their part in the wider Church, seeing decline reversed and wonderful growth in the Church again.

Finally, and perhaps most importantly, an exciting dynamic being seen in resource churches across the country is a determination to prioritise prayer. Many resource churches are very involved in Thy Kingdom Come and the 24-7 Prayer movement, with some churches having dedicated 24-7 prayer rooms. We know from church history that when God stirs churches and individuals to pray over an extended time, especially when they engage in repentance and prayer for those outside the Church, renewal often follows. John Wesley famously said, "God does nothing but in answer to prayer".[181] It feels like a healthy sign where leaders cultivate a dependence on God for something greater, rather than anything that could be achieved on their own. The early church prayed for boldness to speak God's words and to heal and perform signs and wonders through Jesus.[182] This is one response to the 2020s' vision of being a Church that is humbler, bolder and simpler.

Resource churches are indeed an essential part of the Church, with a significant role to play. They have found a new place in an old institution. My hope is that everyone, from bishops to diocesan teams to church leaders to the wider Church, supports them to be the best they can be in order to strengthen the whole Church to the glory of God!

ST GEORGE'S STAMFORD
Diocese of Lincoln

*St George's Stamford is a lively, all-age church in the centre of Stamford in the Diocese of Lincoln. The church was established in the 13th century, and was designated as a resource church in January 2019. St George's purpose is 'making disciples on mission with Jesus' by growing congregations and midweek community groups. It is led by the rector, **Martyn Taylor**, who writes:*

Like many churches, we have always seen ourselves as a resource church because the resources of God's Spirit are at work in us as individuals and as a body. Even before Lincoln Diocese officially designated us as a resource church, we were already doing the work of a resource church. The Holy Spirit empowers us to share the good news of God's kingdom revealed in Jesus Christ in Stamford, the surrounding area, South Lincolnshire, and the ends of the earth.

We see St George's as a pool of water into which God pours the living water of the Holy Spirit; we see ripples of the Spirit's activity emanating out from the centre in concentric circles to create a wider influence for God's kingdom. The first ripple is from the centre. Our central resourcing points are our gathered meetings, midweek and on a Sunday, where we worship God together and encounter his presence through his Word and by his Spirit. Our public gatherings refresh us for our own personal discipleship and growth in obedience and conformity to Christ as we read his Word daily and call out to him in prayer.

The second ripple that pushes out from the centre is our daily interaction with Stamford, sharing God's love, meeting people's needs, introducing people to Jesus. We might think of Christians Against Poverty (CAP), Friday Connect, Street Pastors, Life Skills, Fresh Hope, food bank, schools work, and practical caring for our neighbour. We also think of our networks of relationships at the school gate, sports club, or Weight Watchers, where we engage in verbal witness to the good news of Jesus. The life of the Spirit not only fills us, he pushes us out to be a resource to our immediate community.

Further ripples from our resourcing centre extend to the surrounding area, the local villages and smaller market towns where we come from. Using our homes and community spaces, we work out in a smaller local setting the life of Jesus for the sake of our local community and the growth of his kingdom. As part of our calling to resource the local area and grow disciples, we see a resource church as one which plants more churches. We have a new challenge to resource the larger market towns of South Lincolnshire as part of our vision to plant more churches. The Spirit is pushing some of us out on a wave to carry the good news of Jesus to reach new communities in Grantham and Spalding, using the things that we have learned at St George's to help stimulate new growth in new places for the sake of God's kingdom.

Finally, of course we are committed to world mission through our missions giving and support of our world mission partners. For some of us it means active involvement and interest in overseas visits, building projects, training and equipping others using our skills, intercession and prayer.

We are a resource church by virtue of the work of the Spirit in our midst. Because all believers have received the Spirit, the overflow of the Spirit's work in our own lives enables us to be a resource. *We are resourced to be a resource.*

Our prayer is that as St George's overflows with the life of God's Spirit the ripples of his grace reach out so that many might come to know Jesus in Stamford, the surrounding area, the market towns of South Lincolnshire, and to the ends of the earth.

The Rt Revd Dr David Court, Bishop of Grimsby, Acting Bishop of Lincoln

For us as a diocese, designating three of our churches as resource churches, and then working closely with them to enable them to begin to fulfil that role, was part of a deliberate missional strategy, recognising that in what is seen as a rural diocese, the majority of the population actually live in just 10 'urban' centres, and that church life in the majority of those centres was far from what we would want it to be. Our expectation is to see the three resource churches grow themselves over the next five years, and from that growth strategically plant or revitalise congregations in a further eight of our 'urban' areas.

Asking St George's Stamford to be one of those three key churches was for us an easy decision, recognising that for many years St George's has been one of our strongest church communities with a long history of quietly seeking to do all that we were hoping our resource churches would do. They already had the DNA which sought to give away and resource others, and so have an impact much further than their immediate geographical borders. The designation, along with the extra resources it has enabled us to put into St George's, has meant we have been able to work ever more closely with the leadership of St George's in a focused, strategic way, as we seek together to bring about the growth we long to see.

Two years in, and the early signs are promising! Relationships between St George's and the diocese are probably as strong as they have ever been. Key staff have been and are in the process of being recruited. Two of the urban areas we hope to see revitalised from St George's have been identified. Conversations with the local clergy of those areas have been incredibly positive, with a real desire to work with and benefit from what St George's has to offer for the good of the people in the towns they seek to serve, and we feel that our hopes and plans are slowly beginning to take shape.

It is clearly too early, after only a couple of years of essentially preparing the ground, to make any kind of sensible evaluation of what it is we are trying to do. It is probably true that it has taken longer for us to get to where we are than we originally anticipated, but we are feeling positive and we would do it again. We are still to see the fruit of those revitalised urban areas of our diocese, but the planning and intentionality of purpose of our resource churches, the big vision that seeks to see a kingdom difference and the challenge of being held accountable for the delivery of what it is they say they intend to do, is beginning to have an impact on many other areas of our diocesan life together.

Do we see them as the only way to bring growth and transformation across the diocese? Obviously not, and it has been really important for us to communicate that clearly to all of the other church communities we also want to see making a difference to the people they are there to serve. However, we do believe that resource churches have a vital role as part of what we are trying to do, and we are looking forward and praying expectantly to see what God will do through them in this part of God's world.

AFTERWORD

Sarah Mullaly, Bishop of London

When I was appointed as the Bishop of London in 2018, the description of the early Church after Pentecost stood out to me again and again as I prayed and talked to people inside and outside the church:

> *They devoted themselves to the apostles' teaching and fellowship, to the breaking of bread and the prayers. All who believed were together and had all things in common; they would sell their possessions and goods and distribute the proceeds to all, as any had need. And day by day the Lord added to their number those who were being saved.*

ACTS 2:42-47

This is a beautiful picture of a church that was dynamic, radical, attractive and impactful. No wonder the Lord added to their number day by day!

As we prayed and talked across our diocese, we discerned that God was calling us to a vision *for every Londoner to encounter the love of God in Christ.* It is an ambitious vision that lifts our eyes to all that God calls us to be and to do. *For every Londoner.*

But this is not just for London. The church is for everyone, everywhere. Parishes churches remain at the core of our understanding of how we serve our nation. But other churches are needed to complement them – from network churches to youth congregations to estate churches. Every church has a part to play. And we must continue to pursue a vigorous policy of church planting, whether they are in new contexts or revitalising old ones, wherever mission opportunity arises, and wherever possibilities can be created.

Resource churches have emerged in this context as key enablers of this work, incubating new ministry, refreshing existing ministry, developing multi-site churches, collecting churches together into networks, giving benefits of scale and lay leadership development. They are being established all around the country and they are having a transformative effect. We have already appointed 19 in London and we are keen to continue to encourage them to grow, give away their resources, revitalise parishes and plant new churches. They are playing a key role and will continue to do so.

This book is an important contribution to our understanding of resource churches and the church today. Not only does it describe resource churches in detail and depth, but it provides us with reflection and challenge. Whilst there might be some hesitation in parts of the Church regarding resource churches, they have, as Ric suggests, found a new place in an old institution. These stories of what God is doing give me hope and faith for the future of the gospel in our land. My challenge is, what we can learn from them and this book?

Whilst it is God who added to their numbers those whom he was saving, I am sure it was the intentionality of the early disciples in their following of Jesus and his ways that enabled others to encounter God where his Spirit transformed lives. It is my hope that increasingly more people will encounter the hope that I have found in Jesus Christ and experience his transforming love. Part of our capacity for this transformation lies in resource churches. If we were to see some of the stories described in this book multiply around the country over the coming years, the Church will be a very different place, our communities will be transformed, and more people will encounter the love of Christ I have come to know, not just *for every Londoner,* but for every person, everywhere.

These stories of what God is doing give me hope and faith for the future of the gospel in our land

Jesus is building his Church, growing existing churches and planting new ones.

This new book, written by one of the leading advocates of church planting in England, sets out a broad vision and the essential elements involved in planting new churches.

Including the whys and hows of creating new Christian communities in order to reach new people in new places, this will be a key resource for the emerging vision of a church where different expressions of Christian community are encouraged and supported to flourish.

Coming soon.

CCX.media

CCX.media is a resource hub to inspire, provoke and equip you to multiply.

Every resource we create is now accessible in one place; with hundreds of products and contributors, there is something here for you wherever you are on your planting journey.

Choose the membership option that works for you and get equipped to play your part.

For more information visit ccx.org.uk/ccx-media

VIDEOS

RESOURCES

LIVESTREAMS

COURSES

CONFERENCES

BOOKS

the Gregory
centre for church multiplication

The Gregory Centre for Church Multiplication, known as CCX, supports leaders, church teams and dioceses across London, England and beyond as they multiply disciples, churches and networks.

CCX is led by the Bishop of Islington, the Rt Revd Ric Thorpe. In 2015, Bishop Ric was consecrated as the Bishop of Islington in order to support the Diocese of London's goal of creating new worshipping communities across the capital.

We're part of the Church of England but work with many denominations and networks.

Connect with us by signing up to our newsletter or find out more by visiting ccx.org.uk

A List of Questions for Bishops and Resource Church Leaders

For bishops and diocesan colleagues:	For a church leader and leadership team:
Have you developed a vision and strategy for the diocese/city/town – which includes the role of resource churches?	Have you developed a vision and strategy for planting sustainably? Have you talked to your bishop about it?
How will you communicate this vision to the diocese so that everyone is on board?	How will you communicate this vision to the congregation?
Have you designated one or more churches as resource churches?	Have you built the team needed for the resource church?
Do some need to be planted from scratch? If so, have you identified a leader?	Have you identified a leader and a team for the first plant? What development does your team need?
Have you identified planting opportunities within the diocese/city/town?	Are you working with the diocese on planting opportunities?
Have you allocated planting curates to the resource church?	Do you need to build your 'sending capacity'?
Do you have sufficient resources for the strategy?	Do you have sufficient resources for the plant?
How will you align diocesan policies and practice to the strategy, e.g., to develop a pipeline of future planters?	Do you need to align culture and practice to the church-planting strategy e.g., to develop a pipeline of future leaders and teams?
How do you plan to support your resource church leaders?	How do you plan to support your bishop?

Impact vs Feasibility Matrix Tool for Identifying Planting Priorities

One tool that is helpful for identifying church planting opportunities is to plot where a church currently is in terms of the missional impact they could make, versus how feasible it might be to initiate change right now. This can form the basis for a discussion about the reasons for where it currently is, and the issues surrounding potential planting.

It can be plotted on a simple diagram like the one here. This can be done within a parish or in a diocese on a wider scale.

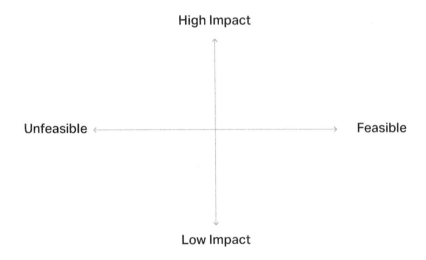

'Stay-in-place' Curacies – Policy Paper in London Diocese

Introduction

A number of churches have requested 'keeping' ordinands and curates through training in order to use them to build growth and deploy them for church planting. This is because they have the vital and hard-won DNA and relationships to persuade people to leave a church in order to plant elsewhere. The comments below are aimed at giving some structure and guidance as to how such training arrangements might work in practice.

Which churches?

Some churches are actively looking to develop leaders to grow their churches and support their mission. In churches where there is high turnover, holding on to leaders becomes important to enable continuity of mission, particularly where church growth and community engagement are changing rapidly. These churches are marked by younger congregations, ongoing church growth, planting new congregations and church planting to other places. The vision and values need to be aligned for trust to be built. Leaders who have grown up through these churches have the trust and understanding developed through working under the oversight of senior leaders over years.

Some churches will encourage ordinands and curates to go elsewhere to get a broader training. Some might not want to continue that leadership relationship. The leaders-in-training themselves might prefer to go elsewhere for their next appointment.

Staying through the next stage of training will be by mutual agreement with the bishop, the incumbent and the candidate. A clear training pathway suitable to the candidate will be identified if the incumbent is keen to retain them.

Which people?

Leaders that fall into this category will self-select. If the incumbent wants to offer them a post for the next stage of training – either as an ordinand, or as a curate – they would ask the bishop for permission, and then make the trainee an offer, subject to the usual conditions. If the trainee wishes to accept, they can do so. If they want to explore other options, they can do this through the usual process of discernment.

What pathway?

The incumbent has an initial conversation with the potential ordinand about staying in the church and joining the staff team. If this is positive, the incumbent asks the bishop to permit the ordinand to stay for training. Once selected, the ordinand is offered a formal place in the 'sending' church. If the ordinand would prefer to go elsewhere, this is worked out with the bishop. Likewise, for ordinands ready to be ordained, the incumbent agrees with the ordinand about staying on, subject to the bishop's affirmation. Once agreed, the church becomes that person's title post.

This approach will need to be fully embraced by Diocesan Directors of Ordinands and Area Directors of Training and Development so that there is no two-tier system but rather a mutually agreed two-track system. Compliance with Post Ordination Training requirements will be required: otherwise, progression to the next stage of training or appointment would be delayed or prevented.

Some exceptional candidates will be capable of being placed in a leadership position in a church plant or new congregation fairly soon after ordination. Supervision arrangements will need to be set in place in such instances.

Strengthening training

Where ordinands and curates stay in their sending church, training will be enhanced through specific periodic (one to four-week) placements to broaden their understanding of the Church of England. Such placements would be encouraged and agreed at the beginning of the training stage. Creative and expanded placements would be arranged in such a way that the timing and experience fulfils the identified requirements.

Lessons Learned in Developing Planting Curates in Leeds Diocese

Selection

As the Diocesan Director of Ordinands[183] better understands the requirements of being a 'planting curate', they can be more readily identified early in the discernment process, and directed towards an appropriate training path.

A key part of the discernment process and subsequent selection as a designated planting curate, is a clear understanding of the person specification (see the job specification in Appendix 5) which describes the essential characteristics to be effective in this role – including an entrepreneurial spirit and proven leadership ability. A candidate who has not had substantial church leadership experience prior to training is likely to struggle.

It may be that a candidate carries a set of expectations and assumptions that need to be challenged. This is a danger of hearing lots of success stories at conferences and leaving with 'romantic' views on reality. Candidates must be prepared for hard work and resilience in the face of failure which is an essential component of any pioneering role.

A plant is likely to require a strong focus on building a community that becomes a church, rather than 'doing church' and expecting people to show up.

Another key requirement is that the candidate is making a longer time commitment which includes their curacy plus two to three years establishing a plant. Whereas other curates looking for their first post may have the flexibility to choose location, a planting curate is making a commitment to the diocese to serve in a plant which is likely to leave them with few options, if any, for their first post.

Training

The job description of a planting curate brings additional challenges onto the training programme to ensure they are appropriately equipped. In summary, they need to have covered all the core ground that any trainee needs, *plus* have additional skills.

Curates that train at a large, well-structured church, and have a well-defined role within the ministry team, may not see the reality of leading a plant where they will be living on the edge of chaos. This is a typical scenario if the curacy is served at a city-centre resource church. This must be addressed during the curacy period with specific training components that may include a placement in a recent plant.

Fundamentally, the curate must complete their training with developed team leadership skills. In most cases they will start with a bigger team than a new vicar might typically have. This includes the ability to delegate, see the big picture, to be an enabler of others, to manage conflict and contrasting personal styles, to adopt a range of leadership styles dependent on the situation.

Due to the fast-paced nature of a plant, they will benefit from strength in change management: goal setting, communication and stakeholder management, rapid decision-making.

Such a rounded training need will be easier to fulfil if the candidate undertakes contextual theological training and is exposed to a range of ministry contexts during their training time.

Job Specification for Planting Curates in Leeds Diocese

Employer: Leeds Diocesan Board of Finance
Job Title: Resource Church 'Planting Curate'
Accountable to: Resource Church Incumbent

Background

The Diocese of Leeds is developing a network of Resource and Resourcing Churches. These churches are being supported and equipped by the diocese for furthering the diocesan vision for *Confident Christians, Growing Churches, Transforming Communities.*

At the heart of this programme is harnessing the potential of Resource Churches to *plant new congregations* and *revitalise existing churches.* This will primarily be achieved by the recruitment and training of 'planting curates'. These curates will be appointed with the expectation that they will move on to revitalise an existing congregation or plant a new one at the end of their curacy. They will be accompanied by a team of lay people from the Resource Church. This pattern was started in 2017 with a plant from the Leeds City Centre Resource Church (St George's) to St Paul's in the suburb of Ireland Wood, accompanied by forty lay people.

The context to which the Planting Curate will move is likely to have significant differences to the Resource Church within which the curacy has been served.

Job description

The Planting Curate will be required to serve their title post within a church that is developing its capacity to function as Resource Church. The curate's formation will fit around the activities and needs of the host Resource Church, as well as the future ministerial requirements of the church context to which they will move at the end of their curacy. It will provide an opportunity to get a broad experience of ministry, to explore what it is to pioneer, to learn how to make disciples of all ages and to lead new initiatives in order to reach a largely unreached city.

Person specification

- Capacity to function effectively within the ecclesial and social context of both the Resource Church and the designated 'plant'.

- Track record in leading pioneering initiatives.

- An entrepreneurial spirit – resilience in the face of failure, curiosity to explore alternatives.

- A passion for spiritual and numerical growth.

- Can establish credibility and has the confidence/conviction to make others follow.

- A flair for engaging, enabling, mobilising – making things happen, and generating momentum.

- Ability to lead teams effectively – delegating to, and enabling, others.

- Capacity to work collaboratively within the church and the local community – managing groups with differing agendas and handling conflict in a positive way with a view to building strong communities beyond the church.

- Experienced in nurturing disciples and with proven potential as an effective teacher.

- Energetic and resilient – able to work in a fast-paced environment and make effective decisions under pressure.

- A person of prayer who stimulates others to pray.

ABOUT THE AUTHOR

Ric Thorpe was appointed as Bishop of Islington in 2015 to oversee the Diocese of London's church planting and church growth work. He also serves the Church of England nationally, supporting bishops, dioceses, church planters and pioneers, to develop church-planting strategies and to plant new worshipping communities to reach new people in new places in new ways. He is the director of the Gregory Centre for Church Multiplication which offers church growth and church-planting training and support for the full breadth of the Church. Ric is Bishops' Advocate for Fresh Expressions and Chair of the Gratitude Initiative and is an assistant bishop in Southwark Diocese. He has a doctorate in church planting from Asbury Theological Seminary and is a tutor in church planting at St Mellitus College, London.

Before his current role, Ric and his wife Louie led a team from Holy Trinity Brompton to plant into St Paul's Shadwell in London's East End where they served for just over a decade. Over this time, the church went on to send four other planting and revitalisation teams to churches in the local area. Ric trained as a chemical engineer and worked in marketing with Unilever before joining the staff of Holy Trinity Brompton. Ric and Louie have three children and live in London. He loves deeply breathing sea air and taking in a long horizon, and better still, being out on the water in a sailing boat.

NOTES

Introduction – Blue Sky Dreams

1 Along with Sandy Millar were Tricia Neill, Executive Director of Alpha International, and Associate Vicar, Miles Toulmin. The culture Sandy created was one of focused, prayerful, hard work with lots of fun.

2 My story is told in Tim Thorlby's report *Love, Sweat and Tears: Church Planting in East London*. Centre for Theology and Community, 2016. http://www.theology-centre.org.uk/wp-content/uploads/2013/04/ChurchPlanting_Final_online.pdf

3 Simple glossary of terms used in this book:

Archbishop: A senior bishop, overseeing an Anglican province; in England there are two, Canterbury and York.

Archdeacon: A senior member of the clergy responsible for an archdeaconry area, responsible for practical, legal and administrative work.

Area bishop: An assistant bishop in a diocese, overseeing clergy in a specific area.

Bishop: A senior member of the clergy.

Curate: An ordained minister who assists an incumbent of a parish.

Diocesan bishop: A bishop with oversight responsibility for a diocese and all the clergy in it.

Diocese: The main pastoral and administrative area in the Church of England, largely following English county boundaries. There are 42 dioceses in the Church of England.

Incumbent: An ordained priest and senior leader of a parish or group of parishes, also called a rector, vicar or priest-in-charge depending on the parish.

Parish: The smallest pastoral area in the Church of England.

PCC: The Parochial Church Council is an executive committee of a parish church.

1 What is a Resource Church?

4 I first wrote about this in Feb. 2014 for the Church Commissioners' Research and Development website in an article called 'City Centre Resource Churches'.

5 The 'Common Fund' or 'parish share' in a Church of England diocese is money given by congregations in every parish to provide and support clergy and to further God's work in every parish across that diocese. These contributions are called the Common Fund because they are made by everyone, for everyone. The Church of England receives no money from the state for mission or ministry.

6 Drummond, Henry. *The Greatest Thing in the World*, Baker Publishing Group, 1880.

7 Alpha is a 10-week introduction to the Christian faith based around watching a talk and being in a small group to discuss and respond at the pace of the group. More details can be found at http://www.alpha.org

8 Matthew Porter describes the ministry of a resource church in his book, *Overflow*, Authentic Media, 2020, based on the Acts of the Apostles and his experience leading The Belfrey, York, which has planted a number of times.

2 Resource Churches – The Story So Far

9 www.htb.org/our-story

10 Quoted from talk notes of the meeting 18 Jan. 2013.

11 Davies, Madeleine. 'London Diocese to Fund 19 Resource Churches', *Church Times*, 23 November 2019.

12 For example by Bristol Diocese.

13 See Bristol Diocese website.

14 Quoted from a briefing paper, 2 Sept. 2014.

15 Church Growth Research Programme Publication

16 Quoted from an email, 31 Mar. 2020.

17 Tim tells the story of St Swithun's in his book, *Lovechurch*, Hodder & Stoughton, 2018.

18 Stuart Murray lists constraints to planting that includes the number of people needing to be sent, finances, pastoral demands and denominational constraints in his book, *Planting Churches: A Framework for Practitioners*, Paternoster Press, 2009, pp. 143–47.

19 Improving the training was the subject of my doctoral research at Asbury Theological Seminary.

20 Church-planting strategy training covers resource churches, revitalisations, planting on estates and other under-reached places, and accelerating the creation of fresh expressions of church. This is covered in material available from the Gregory Centre.

21 When I mention the spouse of an ordained church leader, I am following the ordained leader's preference of introducing their spouse as the overall leader alongside them.

22 King, Rhiannon. *Summary Church Planting Strategy Church of England Birmingham*, 11 Sept. 2018.

23 Strategic Development Funding – consolidated list of projects, www.churchofengland.org, Jan. 2018.

24 https://www.leicester.anglican.org/about-us/resourcing-churches/

25 Davies, Madeleine. 'London Diocese to Fund 19 Resource Churches',

Church Times, 23 November 2019.
26 Diocese of Southwell and Nottingham

3 The Theology Underpinning Resource Churches

27 Marshall, I. Howard. *Acts*. First, IVP Eerdmans, 1980, p. 62.
28 Marshall p. 83.
29 Allen, Roland. *Missionary Methods: St Paul's or Ours?* Eerdmans, 1962, p. 11.
30 Cole, Neil. *Journeys to Significance: Charting a Leadership Course from the Life of Paul*. 1st edition, Jossey Bass, 2011, p. 99.
31 Acts 18:21
32 Wright, N. T. *Colossians and Philemon*. 1st edition, William B Eerdmans Publishing Co, 1996, p. 17.
33 Cole p. 102.
34 Allen p. 62.
35 Cole p. 103.
36 Avis, Paul. *Becoming a Bishop*. Bloomsbury T&T Clark, 2015, p. 29; Cocksworth, Christopher. *Faith and Order Commission*. Feb. 2014, p. 7.
37 House of Bishops. *Church Planting and the Mission of the Church: A Statement by the House of Bishops*. Church of England, June 2018, p. 5, https://www.churchofengland.org/sites/default/files/2018-06/CHURCH PLANTING AND THE MISSION OF THE CHURCH - June 2018_0.pdf
38 First developed by the Anglican Consultative Council in 1984 and adopted by the General Synod of the Church of England in 1996, with the fourth mark added in 2012.
39 Website header at http://www.churchofengland.org
40 Newbigin, Lesslie. 'Can the West Be Converted?' *Princeton Seminary Bulletin*, vol. 6, no. 1, 1985, p. 26.
41 Newbigin, Lesslie. *The Household of God*. 1st edition, SCM Press, 1953, p. 25.
42 Cray et al. The 2004 *Mission-shaped Church* report, p. *xiii*.
43 Avis p. 26.
44 House of Bishops, p. 6.
45 Cray et al, pp. *ix–x*.
46 Green, Beth, et al. *Church Growth in East London: A Grassroots View*. Centre for Theology & Community, 2016, p. 26, http://www.theology-centre.org.uk/wp-content/uploads/2013/04/Church-Growth-digital.pdf.
47 Wright, Christopher. *The Mission of God: Unlocking the Bible's Grand Narrative*. Inter-Varsity Press, 2006, p. 62.
48 Murray, Stuart. *Church Planting: Laying Foundations*. Paternoster Pr, 1998, pp. 57–58.
49 Ellis, Roger, and Roger Mitchell. *Radical Church Planting*. Crossway

Books, 1992, p. 73.

50 Lings, George. *Reproducing Churches*. BRF, 2017, p. 145.

51 Hirsch, Alan, and Jeff Vanderstelt. *Forgotten Ways: Reactivating Apostolic Movements*. 2nd edition, Brazos Press, 2016, p. 63.

52 Matthew 16:18; Acts 2:37,41,47; 5:14; 6:7; 12:24; 13:49; 16:14,;19:20.

53 Church of England. *Breaking New Ground – Church Planting in the Church of England*. 1st edition, Church House Publishing, 1994.

54 *Breaking New Ground*, p. v.

55 Cray et al. pp. *x–xi*.

56 Worthen, Jeremy. *Church Planting: Theology and History*. Church House Internal Paper, 17 Aug. 2017, p. 1.

57 Church of England. *Church Planting and the Mission of the Church – June 2018*, p. 1.

58 Payne, J. D. *Discovering Church Planting*. 1st edition, IVP USA, 2009.

59 Carey, George, and et al. *Planting New Churches*, edited by Bob Hopkins, Eagle, 1991, p. 32.

60 Cray et al. p. 29.

61 Lausanne Movement. 'Gospel Contextualisation Revisited.' *Lausanne Movement*, 21 June 1997, https://www.lausanne.org/content/gospel-contextualisation-revisited

62 Goheen, Michael W. *Introducing Christian Mission Today: Scripture, History and Issues*. IVP Academic, 2014, pp. 283–84.

63 Cray et al. p. 90.

64 Newbigin, Lesslie. *Foolishness to the Greeks: The Gospel and Western Culture*. Reprint edition, SPCK Publishing, 1986.

65 Vanhoozer, Kevin J., editor. *Everyday Theology: How to Read Cultural Texts and Interpret Trends*. Annotated edition, Baker Academic, 2007, p. 8.

66 Watson, David. *Contagious Disciple Making*. Thomas Nelson, 2014, p. 7.

67 Addison, Steve. *Pioneering Movements: Leadership That Multiplies Disciples and Churches*. Inter-Varsity Press, US, 2015, p. 101.

68 Stanley, Linda. 'Local Churches with High Capacity Church Multiplication Centers.' *The Effective Church Group*, http://effectivechurch.com/local-churches-with-high-capacity-church-multiplication-centers/. Accessed 6 Jan. 2020.

69 Lings, George. *Reproducing Churches*. BRF, 2017, p. 228.

70 Carey and et al, *Planting New Churches* p. 26.

71 James, John. *Renewal: Church Revitalisation along the Way of the Cross*. 10Publishing, 2016, pp. 85– 108.

72 Diocese of Worcester. *Resourcing Churches – Diocese of Worcester*. https://www.cofe-worcester.org.uk/mission-and-ministry/resourcing-churches/. Accessed 7 Jan. 2020.

73 Keller, Timothy J. *Center Church*. 1st edition, Zondervan Main, 2012, p. 355.

74 Four generations of leaders are described in 2 Timothy 2:2: Paul, first, invests in Timothy, second, encouraging him to pass on what he has learnt to reliable people, third, who will in turn teach others, fourth.

75 Cole pp. 125–26.

76 Hopkins, Bob, and Freddy Hedley. *Coaching for Missional Leadership*. ACPI, 2008, pp. 131–32.

77 Bevins, Winfield. *Church-Planting Revolution: A Guidebook for Explorers, Planters, and Their Teams*. Seedbed, 2017, p. 118. Bevins offers an assessment at www.churchplantingneq.com

78 Snyder, Howard A. *The Radical Wesley and Patterns for Church Renewal*. Intervarsity Press, 1982, pp. 182–83.

79 Hopkins and Hedley pp. 9,25.

80 www.ccx.org.uk

4 The Historical Foundations of Resource Churches

81 Moorman, John Richard Humpidge. *A History of the Church in England* 3rd edition, Morehouse Publishing, 1980, p. 14.

82 Bede. *The Ecclesiastical History of the English People*, edited by Judith McClure and Roger Collins, Translated by Bertram Colgrave, 2008 edition, OUP Oxford, 2008, p. 113; Moorman pp. 17–18.

83 Finney, John. *Recovering the Past*. Darton Longman & Todd, 2011, p. 31.

84 Moorman p. 29.

85 Finney p. 105.

86 Bede p. 159.

87 Hunter, George G. *The Celtic Way of Evangelism: How Christianity Can Reach the West . . . Again*. Abingdon Press, 2000, p. 37.

88 Finney p. 113.

89 Moorman p. 27.

90 Godfrey, John. *Church in Anglo-Saxon England*. First edition, Cambridge University Press, 1962, pp. 315–17.

91 The minster was called a 'medemra myster,' or minster of middle rank, Godfrey pp. 319–21, 330; Bede p. 345; Blair, John, editor. *Minsters and Parish Churches: The Local Church in Transition, 950–1200*. First edition, Oxford University School of Archaeology, 1988; Moorman p. 28.

92 Moorman p. 59f.

93 Moorman p. 104.

94 Threlfall-Holmes, Miranda. 'Growing the Medieval Church: Church Growth in Theory and Practice in Christendom c.100–c.1500.' *Towards a*

Theology of Church Growth, edited by David Goodhew, 1st edition, Routledge, 2015, pp. 179–95.

95 Keulemans, Michael. *Bishops: The Changing Nature Of The Anglican Episcopate In Mainland Britain*. Xlibris, Corp., 2011.

96 Moorman p. 122.

97 Tanner, Norman, and Sethina Watson. 'Least of the Laity: The Minimum Requirements for a Medieval Christian.' *Journal of Medieval History*, vol. 32, no. 4, Dec. 2006, pp. 395–423, doi:10.1016/j.jmedhist.2006.09.005.

98 Pounds p. 94.

99 Null, Ashley. 'Divine Allurement: Thomas Cranmer and Tudor Church Growth.' *Towards a Theology of Church Growth*, edited by David Goodhew, 1st edition, Routledge, 2015, pp. 197–215.

100 Moorman p. 238.

101 Moorman p. 288.

102 Bevins, Winfield. *Marks of a Movement*. Zondervan Reflective/Seedbed, 2019, p. 52.

103 Snyder, Howard A. *The Radical Wesley and Patterns for Church Renewal*. Intervarsity Press, 1982, p. 75.

104 Wroth, Warwick William. 'Charles James Blomfield (1786–1857).' *Dictionary of National Biography, 188–1900*, vol. 05, Smith, Elder & Co., 1886.

105 Burns, Arthur. 'Anglican Urban Ministry in Bethnal Green.' *From the Reformation to the Permissive Society: A Miscellany in Celebration of the 400th Anniversary of Lambeth Palace Library*, edited by Melanie Barber, Boydell & Brewer, 2010, p. 283.

106 Bevins, 'Nothing New under the Sun.'

107 Snell, K. *Parish and Belonging: Community, Identity and Welfare in England and Wales, 170–1950*. 1st edition, Cambridge University Press, 2009, p. 409–14.

108 Chambers, S. Allen. *History of St Mary Islington*. p. 75.

109 Islington Church Extension Society. *Church Extension, Report of Proceedings at the Inaugural Meeting of the Islington Church Extension Society*. Seeley, Jackson & Halliday, 1857, p. 15.

110 Baker, T. F. T., editor. *A History of the County of Middlesex: Volume VIII: Islington and Stoke Newington Parishes: Islington and Stoke Newington Vol 8*. Victoria County History, 1985, pp. 88–99.

111 Thorlby, Tim. *A Time To Sow*. The Centre for Theology and Community, 2017, http://www.theology-centre.org.uk/wp-content/uploads/2013/04/CTC-Research-Report-9-A-Time-To-Sow-2017online.pdf, p. 90.

112 Burns p. 285.

113 Walford pp. 373–75.

114 Crockfords. *Glossary of Key Terms*. https://www.crockford.org.uk/faq/
glossary-of-key-terms. Accessed 21 Feb. 2020.

115 Elders, Joseph. *20th Century Churches – an Early 21st Century Perspective
| Historic England. historicengland.org.uk*, http://historicengland.org.uk/
whats-new/debate/recent/places-of-worship/20th-century-churches/.
Accessed 6 Apr. 2020.

116 Holy Trinity Brompton now encompasses St Paul's Onslow Square, St
Augustine's Queensgate and St Jude's Courtfield Gardens; Harbour Church
Portsmouth encompasses All Saints Portsmouth, St George's Portsea and St
Albans Copnor; St Thomas Norwich encompasses two other churches too.

117 Bird, Warren, et al. *The Multi-Site Church Revolution: Being One Church
in Many Locations*. Zondervan, 2006.

118 As described by Tim Thorlby, *Love, Sweat and Tears*.

5 The Importance of Resource Churches

119 Emberson, Iain. 'Faith Survey | Christianity in the UK,' https://
faithsurvey.co.uk/uk-christianity.html. Accessed 1 Apr. 2020.

120 Church of England Strategy Unity data.

121 https://www.gov.uk/government/statistics/rural-population-and-
migration/rural-population-201415

122 Church of England Strategy Unity data.

123 See David Goodhew's evaluation of current reasoning that numerical
church growth of local congregations and the multiplication of local
congregations is theologically unnecessary or theologically suspect in his
book *Towards a Theology of Church Growth*, pp. 5–6.

124 Green, Beth, et al. *Church Growth in East London: A Grassroots View*.
Centre for Theology & Community, 2016, p. 52, http://www.theology-centre.
org.uk/wp-content/uploads/2013/04/Church-Growth-digital.pdf

125 Examples of spiritual measurements at a church level are *Natural Church
Development* by Christian Schwarz and the *Emotionally Healthy Church* by
Peter Scazzero.

126 Lifeway Research. *Becoming Five Multiplication Study*. Exponential, 2019,
p. 12, https://exponential.org/resource-ebooks/becoming-five-multiplication-
study/

127 The Grow Course is available online at www.ccx.org.uk/grow

128 Keller, Timothy J. *Center Church*. 1st edition, Zondervan Main, 2012, pp.
360–61.

129 'Cure of souls' comes from the Latin *Cura Animarum* which means the
'care of souls' indicating the ministry by a priest in a parish looking out for
the spiritual life of every person living within its boundaries.

130 Warren, Rick. *The Purpose Driven Church: Every Church Is Big in God's Eyes*. Zondervan, 1995, pp. 32–33.

131 Brierley, Peter. *Capital Growth What the 2012 London Church Census Reveals*. ADBC Publishers, 2014, pp. 7,133–44.

132 Keller p. 362.

133 See www.messychurch.org.uk for more information.

134 Murray, Stuart. *Church Planting: Laying Foundations*. Paternoster Press, 1998, pp. 57–58.

135 Ellis, Roger, and Roger Mitchell. *Radical Church Planting*. Crossway Books, 1992, p. 73.

136 Lings, George. *Reproducing Churches*. BRF, 2017, p. 145.

137 Canon Dr George Lings wrote his 2008 PhD on the nature of the Church being called to reproduce itself and the need to modify itself to do this.

138 Winfield Bevins, *Church-Planting Revolution*, Seedbed, 2017, pp. 67–68.

139 Matthew Porter describes the ministry of a resource church in his book, *Overflow*, based on the Acts of the Apostles and his experience leading The Belfrey, York, which has planted a number of times.

140 Birmingham Diocesan Board of Finance. City Centre Resource Church – Birmingham Diocesan Board of Finance for Bishop's Council Ref: BC.201.5a. 11 Dec. 2014.

141 Porter, Matthew, *Overflow*, pp. 138–44.

142 Thorlby, *Love, Sweat and Tears* p. 57.

143 Acts 16:6-10

6 Creating a Resource Church

144 This chapter summarises some of the training developed since 2011, using experience from the Gregory Centre Plant Course, consulting with bishops in my role as Bishop of Islington.

145 If a parish is paying £20,000 per year into the Common Fund, and parish costs are, say, £70,000, then the parish is being supported by £50,000 per year. Over 10 years, this is £500,000 or £0.5M. A revitalised parish, with a team and support from a resource church, could potentially enable that parish to become self-supporting, covering all its costs.

146 Details can be found at the Gregory Centre website, www.ccx.org.uk.

147 For 'Common Fund' or 'parish share' see note 5 above.

148 Pre-Covid numbers, there were 900 in the church. This figure of 800 members was taken near the end of a year of lockdown.

7 Planting with Resource Churches

149 Suspension of presentation is the temporary removal of a Patron's right to present an incumbent to a benefice. The Bishop is likely to seek to suspend the rights of presentation to a benefice when, for pastoral, missional or financial reasons, pastoral reorganisation is under consideration. The Bishop remains responsible and licenses a priest-in-charge as a temporary measure.
150 Parish share is where churches give back to their diocese to support the costs of ministry across all the churches. Some give more, some are only able to give less, with the overall aim that costs are covered.

8 Developing Leaders for Resource Churches

151 Currently Tim Keller's paper on Leadership and Church Size Dynamics is here: https://seniorpastorcentral.com/wp-content/uploads/2016/11/Tim-Keller-Size-Dynamics.pdf
152 St Mellitus College and St Hild College both have church planting courses and options; and the Gregory Centre team regularly visits and connects with other Anglican theological colleges.
153 https://stgs.org.uk/internship
154 https://www.youngerleadershipcollege.org
155 Lings, George, *The Day of Small Things*, Church Army report, p. 80.
156 https://www.churchofengland.org/about/policy-and-thinking/our-views/race-and-ethnicity
157 https://www.london.anglican.org/support/ministry-and-vocations/christian-vocation/the-peter-stream
158 https://www.htb.org/leadership-development
159 Doctoral research by Christian Selvaratnam, director of church planting at St Hild College, into comparing craft guilds apprentices with church planting training opens up a more focused approach to training planting curates.
160 Details can be found at the Gregory Centre website, www.ccx.org.uk.
161 The Leadership Pipeline is widely used in business and the charity sector and increasingly in churches. See https://leadershippipelineinstitute.com for more details.

9 Objections and Obstacles

162 Objections are summarised from many conversations over the last five years and explored in training sessions with diocesan senior teams. Obstacles that must be addressed and overcome to create church-planting opportunities for resource churches are taken from my doctoral research findings.

163 See www.renovare.org and Foster, Richard J. *Streams of Living Water: Celebrating the Great Traditions of Christian Faith*, HarperOne Revised edition, 2001.

164 See Jackson, Bob, *Hope for the Church*, CHP 2002, chapter 14, and *The Road to Growth*, CHP 2005, chapter 3.

165 St Paul's Shadwell went through four or five physical transformations mirroring changing church traditions over 350 years, including a major reworking by Butterfield in the 1880s that changed yet again a generation later.

166 St Peter's Bethnal Green and St John-at-Hackney are two with which I am familiar in London Diocese.

167 Temple, William. Recalled as a personal dictum in 'Letter from the Archbishop of the West Indies' in *Theology* (1956), vol. 59.

168 Hebrews 10:24–25.

169 For example, I had helpful conversations with many local church leaders hosted by the bishop in Portsmouth before Harbour Church was planted and St Jude's Southsea kindly invited the new resource church leader to preach to their church about the plant.

170 According to Olly Ryder, this happened when they planted St Matt's Plymouth and local church reinvested in their welcome teams, websites and missional structures, leading to growth and greater missional strength. Relationships remained strong.

171 See www.newlifecommunity.church/restart for more information.

172 Pounds, N. J. G. *A History of the English Parish: The Culture of Religion from Augustine to Victoria*. Revised edition, Cambridge University Press, 2008, p. 94.

173 Keulemans, Michael. *Bishops: The Changing Nature Of The Anglican Episcopate In Mainland Britain*. Xlibris, Corp., 2011 (ch3) describes Bishop Grosseteste's two-year visitation to renew the Lincoln Diocese in 1246 that came into collision with local barons who did not like the church exercising its right to override civil practices.

174 Burns, Arthur. 'Anglican Urban Ministry in Bethnal Green.' *From the Reformation to the Permissive Society: A Miscellany in Celebration of the 400th Anniversary of Lambeth Palace Library*, edited by Melanie Barber, Boydell & Brewer, 2010, p. 283.

175 The Diocesan Advisory Committee or DAC is concerned with the Care of Churches in a diocese. It advises parishes and others on church buildings and works to them, ranging from a major extension to the installation of a new light fitting, reordering the church interior or repairing the roof. This includes advice to the Chancellor on granting permissions through the faculty system.

176 Baker, T. F. T., editor. *A History of the County of Middlesex: Volume VIII: Islington and Stoke Newington Parishes: Islington and Stoke Newington Vol 8.* Victoria County History, 1985, pp. 88–99 and Burns p. 285.
177 Garrison, David. *Church Planting Movements: How God Is Redeeming a Lost World.* Wigtake Resources, 2003 (chapter 5).
178 See www.wearewoven.church
179 Newbigin, Lesslie, *The Open Secret: An Introduction to the Theology of Mission.* 2nd edition, SPCK Publishing, 1995, p. 124.

11 The Future of Resource Churches in the Church of England

180 There are approximately 12,500 parishes in England. If 80 per cent were to plant a church of some kind, small or big, then that would be 10,000 new Christian communities.

12 Conclusion

181 Wesley, John. *A Plain Account of Christian Perfection.* HardPress, 2018, chapter 11.5
182 Acts 4:23–31.
183 A Diocesan Director of Ordinands (DDO) is appointed by the Bishop to oversee the process of selecting, training, choosing and ordaining new ministers into the Church of England.

Printed in Great Britain
by Amazon